The Hatherleigh Guide

to

Vocational and Career Counseling

The Hatherleigh Guides series

The Hatherleigh Guide

to

Vocational and
Career Counseling

Hatherleigh Press • New York

The Hatherleigh Guide to Vocational and Career Counseling

Project Editor: Joya Lonsdale
Indexer: Angela Washington-Blair, PhD
Cover Designer: Gary Szczecina
Cover photo: Christopher Flach, PhD

© 1997 Hatherleigh Press
A Division of The Hatherleigh Company, Ltd.
1114 First Avenue, Suite 500, New York, NY 10021-8325

This book is printed on acid-free paper.

Compiled under the auspices of the editorial boards of *Directions in Mental Health Counseling*, *Directions in Clinical Psychology*, and *Directions in Rehabilitation Counseling*.

Library of Congress Cataloging-in-Publication Data

The Hatherleigh guide to vocational and career counseling —1st ed.
        p.   cm. — (The Hatherleigh guides series; 9)
        Includes bibliographical references and index.
        ISBN 1-886330-50-6 (alk. paper)
        1. Vocational guidance—Handbooks, manuals, etc.
          I. Hatherleigh Press. II. Series.
        RC456.H38 1996 vol.9
        [HF5381]
        616.89 s—dc21   96-50304
        [362.2'04256]   CIP

First Edition: March 1997

10 9 8 7 6 5 4 3 2 1

About the photograph and the photographer

Maretta, Ohio, 1979
Wispy clouds stretch across the summer sky.

Christopher Flach, PhD, is a psychologist in private practice in southern California. An avid photographer for more than 20 years, his favorite subjects include people and nature. He has studied photography with Ansel Adams, and his work has been on display in public galleries and in private collections.

Compiled under the auspices of the editorial boards of *Directions in Mental Health Counseling, Directions in Clinical and Counseling Psychology,* and *Directions in Rehabilitation Counseling:*

Gary Holmes, PhD, CRC
Emporia State University (Emporia, KS)

John Homlish, PhD
The Menninger Clinic (Topeka, KS)

Sharon E. Robinson Kurpius, PhD
Arizona State University (Tempe, AZ)

Marilyn J. Lahiff, RN, CRRN, CIRS, CCM
Private practice (Englewood, FL)

Chow S. Lam, PhD
Illinois Institute of Chicago (Chicago, IL)

Paul Leung, PhD, CRC
University of Illinois at Urbana-Champaign (Champaign, IL)

Carl Malmquist, MD
University of Minnesota (Minneapolis, MN)

Robert J. McAllister, PhD
Taylor Manor Hospital (Ellicott City, MD)

Richard A. McCormick, PhD
Cleveland VA Medical Center-Brecksville Division (Cleveland, OH)

Thomas Miller, PhD, ABPP
University of Kentucky College of Medicine (Lexington, KY)

Jane E. Myers, PhD, CRC, NCC, NCGC, LPC
University of North Carolina-Greensboro (Greensboro, NC)

Don A. Olson, PhD
Rehabilitation Institute of Chicago (Chicago, IL)

William Pollack, PhD
McLean Hospital (Belmont, MA)

Keith M. Robinson, MD
University of Pennsylvania (Philadelphia, PA)

Susan R. Sabelli, CRC, LRC
Assumption College (Worcester, MA)

Gerald R. Schneck, PhD, CRC-SAC, NCC
Mankato State University (Mankato, MN)

George Silberschatz, PhD
University of California-San Fransisco (San Fransisco, CA)

David W. Smart, PhD
Brigham Young University (Provo, UT)

Julie F. Smart, PhD, CRC, NCC
Utah State University (Logan, UT)

Joseph Stano, PhD, CRC, LRC, NCC
Springfield College (Springfield, MA)

Anthony Storr, FRCP
Green College (Oxford, England)

Hans Strupp, PhD
Vanderbilt University (Nashville, TN)

Retta C. Trautman, CCMHC, LPCC
Private practice (Toledo, OH)

Patricia Vohs, RN, CRRN, CRC, CIRS, CCM
Private practice (Warminster, PA)

William J. Weikel, PhD, CCMHC, NCC
Morehead State University (Morehead, KY)

Nona Leigh Wilson, PhD
South Dakota State University (Brookings, SD)

Table of Contents

Illustrations

Introduction

The media speak of the rapid changes the world is undergoing as we enter a new millennium. The fields of vocational and career counseling are no exception. Medical advances that allow more individuals with disabilities to work, changes in legislation (such as the Americans with Disabilities Act), labor market conditions, assistive technology in the workplace, changes in the demographic make-up of our nation — these are just some of the changes that are influencing the services that professionals provide. These societal changes demand a response from vocational rehabilitation professionals and career counselors. *The Hatherleigh Guide to Vocational and Career Counseling* equips them with the information they need to meet this demand.

Today, more than one in five children in the United States lives in poverty (Snyder & Shafer, 1996). Clearly, there is a need for better integration of people into successful and meaningful work roles. However, human services professionals are not given sufficient education and training to meet the challenge of helping clients achieve lifelong career success in today's work climate. Therefore, it is important for mental health professionals to read books like this one to be able to provide the best service possible to their clients.

Work provides more than financial independence and security. Successful work experience confers adult status and acts as one of the "central organizers" in an individual's life. It contributes to a person's sense of identity ("You are what you do"). Work gives a sense of affiliation, belonging, and fulfilling one's duty. In addition, work can provide important social relationships; a sense of prestige, recognition, and status; and a structure for the allocation of time, energy, and resources. Work also often has idiosyncratic rewards — rewards that are unique to each individual. Moreover, meaningful work allows a person to use his or her creativity and spurs growth, stimulation, and self-development. Finally, satisfying, successful vocational functioning improves functioning in other areas of the individual's life.

The benefits of work for individuals with disabilities are significant; in addition to the benefits for all persons, work can help individuals with disabilities achieve mastery, integrate into the broader culture, and achieve independence. Unfortunately, however, in the vocational and career counseling professions, career choice theory, vocational counseling, and career planning have been viewed as having little relevance and applicability for clients with disabilities. Professionals have wrongly assumed that individuals with disabilities must be satisfied with whatever jobs they can get.

Many myths have contributed to a lack of vocational counseling services for clients with disabilities. These include the misconception that the disability itself is the most important determinant of career choice; and the assumptions that career development of individuals with disabilities proceeds at a slower pace, often is unpleasant and stressful, and frequently results in failure. Furthermore, the degree to which conditions are disabling and the need for workplace accommodations often are exaggerated and overestimated. *The Hatherleigh Guide to Vocational and Career Counseling* dispels these myths. To address the issues that have been largely overlooked in the literature, six chapters of this guide explicitly focus on offering clear, practical guidelines for vocational counseling services for individuals with disabilities.

This guide also clearly demonstrates that vocational/career counseling is not the domain of only one or two professions. Readers will get a clear view of the blending of the roles of occupational therapists, mental health counselors, vocational evaluators, psychologists, neuropsychologists, and vocational rehabilitation counselors in helping to provide successful and satisfying work lives for their clients. In addition, several authors outline ways in which professionals from various disciplines can collaborate to provide the best possible outcomes for clients.

Each chapter is written by a professional(s) with expertise in the topic of the chapter and is designed to provide the latest information in professional practice. The combination of information in these twelve chapters brings under one cover a set of related, yet individually important, job placement techniques and vocational and career counseling theories.

Three chapters focus on career counseling and career choice theories and techniques. Chapter 1 by Garrett McAuliffe challenges the traditional concept of *career* as a fixed decision made once in a person's life. McAuliffe presents research on neo-Piagetian cognitive developmental theory, which accounts for the different changes individuals make though the life cycle and the cognitive processes that either enable or disable them from managing the challenges of a career. This theory views *career* as a lifelong series of choices that reflect the changing needs of the individual. The chapter focuses on one developmental theory, that of Robert Kegan, which recognizes personal development to be a "meaning constitutive activity"; as people move though various stages of life, they develop a greater understanding and sense of individuation from the world. McAuliff shows the wide range of career development strategies that are possible with Kegan's approach.

Who has not experienced the anxiety that accompanies life transitions, including career change? In Chapter 2, Lewis Patterson reminds us that "career decisions. . . are not simple, unencumbered, rational experiences—even in the most predictable of circumstances" (p. 18). Patterson identifies six specific fears that may accompany career development and shows how these anxieties may evoke resistance to counseling. He presents a three-stage model of counseling to address client resistance and uses cases to illustrate the application of these techniques.

Chapter 10 by Jay Rojewski discusses the need for an awareness of cultural diversity in career counseling. Largely due to demographic changes in the United States, mental health professionals are working with increasing numbers of clients from ethnic, racial, and cultural minority backgrounds. He highlights the four major racial/ethnic minority groups in the

United States—African Americans, Hispanics, Asians, and Native Americans—and describes the concepts of disability and career development unique to each. Rojewski gives guidelines for goal setting, vocational assessment, and counseling. He also offers valuable insights into the need for sensitivity in accepting different views of the meaning and role of work among minorities. For example, Asian and Native American cultures have a more extrinsic and practical view of careers than does the dominant (i.e., Euro-American) culture and clients from these cultural backgrounds may not view a career as an issue of self-concept and self-actualization.

In addition to Rojewski's helpful discussion of concepts of disability in various cultures, six chapters present much needed guidelines and theory for providing services to individuals with disabilities. Since the Americans with Disabilities Act (ADA) was passed in 1991, rehabilitation workers have had the responsibility to incorporate ADA guidelines into vocational assessments. Chapter 3 by Stephen Thomas outlines the key components of successful ADA-based vocational diagnosis, assessment, and evaluation.

In Chapter 4, Margaret Nosek and Catherine Clubb Foley give clear and practical answers to questions about personal assistance. This information is vital for the estimated 7.7 million individuals in the United States who require some form of personal assistance, as well as for their caretakers. Personal assistance is a "linchpin service" in meeting the survival and productivity needs of people with extensive limitations. Seven major options for sources of personal assistance are discussed and evaluated. The authors make six recommendations for the improvement of personal assistance arrangements, each of which enhances employability.

David Vandergoot, in Chapter 5, explains the concepts and practices that underlie job placement of persons with disabilities. He demonstrates how professionals can help clients by providing rehabilitation services to employers. Using labor market concepts, Vandergoot shows how job placement and employer needs interact.

In Chapter 6, James Schaller, Edna Mora Szymanski, and

Cheryl Hanley-Maxwell present the background, historical development, and core features of supported employment. The authors outline a procedure for assessing both the person and the potential work site and offer techniques for reducing discrepancies between the worker and work environment. Finally, they present a comprehensive input-process-output model for enhancing the quality of supported employment.

Chapter 7 by Rock Weldon and Gary Sigmon describes work hardening, one of the fastest growing fields in health care today. Work hardening is defined as "the rehabilitation of injured workers with the goal of improving their physical abilities so that they are capable of returning to work" (p. 128). A comparison of the "patient personality" and the "worker personality" demonstrates the need to help clients become productive workers. Three work hardening models are presented: (a) sports medicine/exercise, (b) work activity, and (c) integrated vocational/interdisciplinary.

Our own research, presented in Chapter 11, focuses on the vocational evaluation of Hispanic clients with disabilities. This client population presents specific challenges to the vocational evaluator. We outline five problem areas, along with their possible solutions and guidelines for practice: (a) complexity of defining Hispanic populations, (b) inequitable employee selection, (c) inappropriate test content, (d) inappropriate test standardization, and (e) language bias. It is important to work with the challenges of diversity; thorough and accurate multicultural evaluations are more economical in the long run.

Two chapters address the vocational evaluation and rehabilitation of patients with special medical or psychiatric conditions that present specific challenges to obtaining and maintaining work. In Chapter 8, Robert Fraser discusses the three levels of vocational evaluation of clients with traumatic brain injury (TBI). A case study illustrates proper vocational evaluation techniques. Fraser gives helpful suggestions for working with other professionals such as speech pathologists and neuropsychologists.

Chapter 9 deals with vocational rehabilitation of patients

with schizophrenia. The authors, H. Richard Lamb and Cecile Mackota, give a rationale for work therapy for patients with schizophrenia. Work therapy may well be more helpful than a regimen of day activity and is within the reach of many individuals with schizophrenia. The concepts that underlie work therapy include (a) the satisfaction of mastery, (b) establishing high but realistic expectations, and (c) the fact that work is a valued social role in our culture and is an indication of normalcy.

The closing chapter appropriately addresses improving the delivery of rehabilitation services for all the client populations discussed in this book. Chapter 12 by Stephen Thomas outlines the primary considerations for systematically choosing appropriate vocational evaluation services, determining client readiness for referral, writing objective referral questions, and using evaluation reports in effective rehabilitation planning.

The Hatherleigh Guide to Vocational and Career Counseling provides a much needed resource for all mental health professionals who encounter issues surrounding work in their practices, especially those with vocational rehabilitation and career development specialties. This book will help these professionals address the current societal need for the better use of America's human resources. Perhaps most important, this book will facilitate the realization of more fulfilling and meaningful vocational lives for clients with a variety of needs at the individual level.

Julie F. Smart, PhD, CRC, NCC,
LPC, ABDA
Logan, Utah

David W. Smart, PhD
Provo, Utah

Dr. Julie Smart is Assistant Professor in the Department of Special Education and Rehabilitation, Utah State University, Logan, UT. Dr. David Smart is Professor at the Counseling and Development Center, Brigham Young University, Provo, UT.

REFERENCE

Snyder, T., & Shafer, L. (1996). *Youth indicators, 1996.* Washington, DC: U.S. Department of Education, National Center for Education Statistics.

1

A Constructive Developmental Perspective on Career Counseling

Garrett McAuliffe, PhD

Dr. McAuliffe is Associate Professor of Counselor Education at Old Dominion University, Norfolk, VA.

KEY POINTS

- Traditionally, *career* has been defined as a static, fixed, one-time decision, usually made in late adolescence or early adulthood. However, new theories recognize *career* to be a lifelong series of choices that people make to express their changing needs.

- Most career-phase theories do not explain cognitive processes that enhance or diminish a person's ability to manage career challenges. Emerging neo-Piagetian cognitive theories of adult development, however, can account for these processes.

- This chapter explores Robert Kegan's cognitive developmental theory, which provides what may be the most comprehensive, broadly applicable explanation of personality development available.

- Kegan's theory explains how the self constructs meaning across the affective, cognitive, and moral domains by making a succession of qualitative differentiations of the self from the world.

- Three structures characterize an adult's meaning construction, each of which is progressively more adequate for confronting the lack of stability inherent in any career: the interpersonal balance, the institutional balance, and the interindividual balance.

- Seemingly simple transitions can be opportunities for deep structural transformation. The counselor's tasks are to assess clients' implicit meaning-making stances and challenge and support clients to face dilemmas and become open to new possibilities.

INTRODUCTION

Career has been defined in recent years as a lifelong series of choices that persons make to express their changing needs (Greenhaus, 1987). Consistent with this trend, current theories describe career in terms of the sequential phases through which all workers pass.

This dynamic understanding of *career* has replaced the static conception that had been a legacy of the trait–factor-dominated counseling approach. In the static view, career choice was seen as a relatively fixed, one-time decision, usually made in late adolescence or early adulthood. Trait–factor-oriented counselors merely attempted to match the individual's characteristics (traits) with equivalent conditions (factors) in occupations. A good lifetime career match was the goal for this type of counseling. However, when it was discovered that career change was more the norm than the exception, simple matching theory was no longer adequate.

Newer descriptions of career phases can help counselors and clients identify tasks that promote successful adaptation throughout life. However, although most career-phase theories name the typical tasks and issues that characterize each phase, they do not generally explain the cognitive processes that enhance or diminish a person's ability to manage the challenges of a career. On the other hand, emerging cognitive theories of adult development are grounded in the description of the "knowledge structures" and "meaning-making balances." These were posited by Piaget (1970) and define approaches to problem solving.

This chapter explores the career counseling implications of one cognitive developmental theory in particular—the constructive developmental theory of Robert Kegan (1982). Kegan's theory is perhaps the most comprehensive, broadly applicable explanation of personality development available. Unlike theories that restrict themselves to the moral or educational domains, Kegan's theory applies to the full range of human endeavors, including family relationships, leadership, and, in this case, career. From this perspective, a client's meaning-making framework, or constructive developmental stage, contributes significantly to the ability to adapt to career challenges.

CONSTRUCTIVE DEVELOPMENT

Kegan's constructive developmental theory is perhaps the most inclusive of the cognitive-developmental theories. It explains how the self constructs meaning across the affective, cognitive, and moral domains. Kegan describes development as a "meaning-constitutive activity"; that is, as people move through what are variously called "stages" or "balances in subject-object relations," they achieve more expansive, inclusive understandings of themselves and the world. In Kegan's terms, constructive development is a succession of qualitative differentiations of the self from the world, or seeing oneself as distinct from the world. At each succeeding stage, the person is able to include more of the world as "object." Each constructive developmental stage is a successive triumph of "relationship to" other things in the world rather than "embeddedness in" the world.

Kegan suggests that three such structures characterize most adults' meaning construction: (a) the interpersonal balance, (b) the institutional balance, and (c) the interindividual balance. It should be noted, however, that most persons' meaning-making is not likely to be fully characterized by one balance; rather, it is likely to have characteristics of two balances, with one predominating.

The Interpersonal Balance:

The interpersonal balance is typical of most adolescents and some adults. Those who make meaning from the interpersonal perspective are embedded in their relationships with others; they cannot generate a perspective outside the relationships in which they live. As such, the interpersonally embedded client is "pieced out" to his or her reference groups – peers, parents, and political and religious groups. In the interpersonal balance, one might say, "I *am* my relationships," rather than, "I have relationships." Rather than embarking on an authentic quest to express who he or she is, the interpersonally balanced client searches for the path of least resistance – the one that has been well travelled or highly recommended, perhaps by his or her family or peers. The interpersonal self is not individuated sufficiently to possess a coherent identity.

Although basic research on this relatively new theory is still underway, two studies (Bar-Yam, 1991; McAuliffe & Neukrug, 1992) found that 45%–53% of persons over the age of 21 make meaning largely from the interpersonal balance. It follows that many of these persons make career choices based on unquestioned assumptions about the appropriate fields and roles for someone in their reference group – be it family, ethnicity, class, or religious group.

The blind allegiance of the interpersonal balance can have unfortunate consequences. For example, a 30-year-old woman insisted to her counselor that she enroll in a demanding computer training program, despite a seeming lack of aptitude in that area, because her family members had recommended that field. One year later, after she found herself on academic probation, she was helped by her counselor to act on her own voice, which called her to early childhood work. Such is the power and the danger of operating within the interpersonal balance.

The Institutional Balance:

The limits of the interpersonal balance are reached if the environment challenges the client to generate a point of view. For many people, college provides such an environment, one in which the conflicting voices of professors, peers, parents, and others become a cacophony. The only escape from such an environment is finding a center in oneself, a place where the self can be first discovered, and then expressed, through opinions, ideologies, and, most important, career goals.

The strength of the institutional self strength lies in its ability to identify its own purposes and articulate a position independently; that is, to run itself as a somewhat fixed institution. The institutionally balanced client typically pursues a career singlemindedly and is intent on being "a force to be reckoned with." This self-authored voice allows one to speak from one's own center; to discover new and old needs, values, and interests; and ultimately to act in a relatively autonomous fashion. As a client once said, "I used to try to be whatever I thought was the right way to be — which was what my family had communicated. That cut me off from the creative, expressive me I'm now letting out!" The refrain of the institutional balance might be, "You can't please everyone, so you've got to please yourself."

Although the independent, self-assertive mode of the institutional balance is a triumph over the stifling externality of interpersonalism, it can also be a powerful limitation; in the institutional balance, the person lacks the capacity for self-correction and reflection on the fundamental purposes of the forms (e.g., occupation, other life roles, political or religious affiliations) that express those purposes.

In essence, a client who operates from the institutional perspective declares, "I *am* my occupation" rather than, "I have an occupation." This identification limits the client to making the continued maintenance of the self as an institution the very goal of the institutional self; self-perpetuation in a current form (e.g. secretary, electrician, homemaker) thus becomes an end in itself. In the institutional balance, the authentic career quest can be stymied by the client's rigidity by being closed to new expressions of the self. This embeddedness in the particular life role, or the "form" one has taken, does not allow either for self-correction or for the understanding that one's career quest should be undertaken with respect to the larger purposes (e.g., principles, values) of which career is merely a present expression.

Such blindness to one's larger potentials can result in career distress until a more flexible balance is achieved.

One of my clients, Ken, had singlemindedly pursued a retail sales career for which he was poorly suited. Ken had been let go twice for being ineffective at selling. However, he continued his pursuit because, in his words, "I've always thought of myself as a salesperson in a retail setting. It's what I've always been." In his institutional embeddedness, Ken was thoroughly identified with the form (the retail sales role) rather than with larger purposes that had been hidden by the blind adherence to a questionable goal. Through counseling, Ken was able to reflect on his larger values and to recognize his actual abilities, which were better suited to technical vocations. His personal revolution resulted in successful entry into computer repair work and also in a broader perspective for the future on his evolving self.

The Interindividual Balance:

As the case of Ken illustrates, development beyond the institutional balance can be described as movement in which the self no longer *is* its particular form but instead *has* forms and is "more committed to culturing a process than preserving a product." The interindividual balance is characterized by openness to new information that may challenge the form (e.g., occupation) that one may have already accepted. In the interindividual balance, any predetermined orientation to conflict and information is transcended, allowing the client to hear dissonant voices and *invite* contradiction, as opposed to preserving its own coherence at all cost.

Basseches (1984) proposes that "dialectical thinking," which is characterized by openness to contradiction and flexible movement through particular forms, is a major asset in negotiating life choices and transitions because it gives people the greatest number of options for responding to their internal needs and the external environment. According to Kegan, the interindividual balance similarly allows people to be self-transforming — open to new expressions of their yearnings and responsive to internal and external reports on their performance, their likes, their impact on others, and their changing needs. Such flexibility makes the interindividual balance appealing as a framework from which to manage career transition.

The interindividual balance may be especially advantageous for negotiating adult redefinitions of self, as in mid-life and beyond, because it is characterized by self-reflectiveness, the welcoming of contradictions, and acceptance of incompleteness. Fortunately, Ken was counseled to question the necessity of his being a salesperson and, more significantly, to rethink the limiting, relatively fixed way that he was making meaning in general. As he was challenged to broaden his occupational identity, he began to step — tentatively and fearfully — in new directions, as evidenced by a return to technical work and even consideration of a computer design career.

INCREASING ADEQUACY AND DEVELOPMENT

Each of the aforementioned balances is succeedingly more adequate for confronting the lack of stability inherent in career and for being responsive to change. The interpersonally balanced client cannot easily act on internal cues to make changes; in fact, this person cannot even identify a self from which to speak. Similarly, although those in the institutional balance do pursue a self-authored track, they can easily get stuck on a one-way, narrow path and are unable to hear negative reports, both internal and external; therefore, they may be incapable of imagining options beyond those boundaries.

In contrast, the person in the interindividual balance has an advantage in facing transitions, in making minor or major career shifts, in redefining the self, and in accommodating to the sometimes dissonant reports of the world. This person seeks out newness and contradiction, and thus is ready for the discovery of new paths or the transformations that the career quest inevitably requires. In this way, each developmental balance is more adaptive in that it allows more information to be included in the resolution of career dilemmas.

From the constructive developmental perspective, the manner in which persons address career concerns will vary according to the epistemologic framework from which the person speaks. The person who is operating from an interpersonal balance wonders, "What does my community, my family, or my ethnic or religious group expect of me?" and the person with an institutional perspective asks, "How do I maintain the current form I am in?" In contrast, the central career questions for the interindividual perspective are, "Who am I becoming?" and, "How shall I express this emerging self?" For many adults, the interindividual perspective can provide the readiness to redefine the self in more comprehensive ways. This perspective may be particularly important for addressing the changes in meaning in adulthood that may happen at mid-career or at other times.

COUNSELING FOR TRANSITION AND TRANSFORMATION

Counseling strategies based on a constructive-developmental perspective will depend on the nature of the change that is mandated. A career dilemma may trigger either simple *transition*, such as a job change, or *personal transformation* — a substantial shift in the very definition of one's self. For example, Ken experienced both transition and transformation in his occupational change from retail work to computer repair work. His transformation was exemplified in his statement that "I always thought it was necessary to be certain and committed, even singleminded, in my ambitions. In the process, I ignored my own doubts, couldn't hear others' voices, and left out significant dimensions of myself." Counselors can help with transition and transformation if they are able to assess a client's current dominant meaning-making framework and then provide a challenging yet supportive environment for change.

ASSESSING CONSTRUCTIVE DEVELOPMENT

Assessment of the client's meaning-making system, or developmental level, is a task of the early phase of developmentally oriented career counseling. The goal of such assessment is to determine whether constructive transformation or, alternatively, surface adjustments within a particular constructive developmental stage should be addressed. However, it should be noted that seemingly superficial change can also be an opportunity for constructive development. As developmentally alert counselors establish a relationship with the client, they can assess the client's current balance from informal interview data or by means of the subject-object interview. Questions such as, "What would be your cost in changing fields?" or, "How do you know that this is the right decision for you?" evoke constructive developmental information. Clues such as reliance on outside sources for approval (the interpersonal) or a singular, closed pursuit of a career goal (the institutional) may indicate the current dominant meaning-making framework.

DEFINING THE COUNSELING OBJECTIVE

In some cases, simple transition from one occupational role to another may seem most appropriate. For example, if a 20-year-old client seems to recognize and act on her own needs (a quality of the institutional balance) or if the potential mid-life career changer reveals a flexible definition of self (an element of the interindividual balance), occupational change should be the focus of counseling. Such transition might be effected with a combination of reflective clarification, information giving, encouragement, and use of a rational decision-making strategy.

In contrast, when the meaning-making system seems to be inadequate to the transition task, the counselor should help clients discover "what they don't know they don't know." The client may need to be guided to powerful learning experiences that are transforming, to change not just what is known, but *how* he or she knows. Clients frequently come to counselors with stirrings of personal revolutions and sometimes ideas of how transformation might occur, however inarticulate these may be. In such cases, it is the counselor's challenge to assist clients in their transformations of meaning-making.

When transformation is required, the career counselor's job is more than that of an information provider whose aim might be to help the client accumulate more knowledge about self and the world. In many cases, both transition and transformation can be blended, as counselor and client set tentative goals of both rethinking the client's usual way of making meaning (for transformation) and exploring information about the self and occupations (for transition).

A FRAMEWORK FOR TRANSITION AND TRANSFORMATION

The counselor might use Loder's framework of five "moments" in personal transformation (1989) as a guide for simple change or for the reconstruction of meaning. In Loder's model, the counselor encourages the client to experience five "transforming moments":

1. *Conscious conflict* — facing dissatisfactions and dilemmas squarely

2. *Pause* — giving time and energy to the implications of the conflict

3. *Image* — vividly experiencing the implications of the conflict in a new or renewed commitment

4. *Repatterning* — fleshing out the image

5. *Interpretation* — acting on the decision

The focus of Loder's model on conflict holding is consistent with the disequilibration that Piaget suggests is central to developmental change. Illustrations of constructive-developmental career counseling in two adult stages follow.

Transformation from the Interpersonal Balance:

In the interpersonal balance, the counselor's challenge is to ask relationship-embedded clients to make their own new career meanings. Activities that promote movement from the interpersonal to the institutional balance are accomplished by the counselor's challenging the client to discover and act on information about the self. Such discovery might be triggered by various self-exploration activities, in which the client is asked to consider and generate the implications of his or her abilities, interests, and values. The counselor should highlight contradictions between self-assessed needs and the person's current life roles and activities. In these ways, stage-embedded assumptions about who is in charge of career can be challenged.

For example, for the young adult college student whose seemingly simple dilemma is to choose between pursuing a parent-approved premedical track or to consider the internal voice that draws her to the social sciences, counseling would operate on two levels: one to weigh the pros and cons of various fields of study and the other to support and challenge the person so that the tacit assumptions about "who's in charge" become conscious. A counselor who focuses only on psychosocial issues in this case might emphasize the exploratory trying-on of occupations and the seeking of appropriate information. If the client were left with meaning derived from other sources, a rich opportunity to assist in a framework shift would have been missed; this change, in the cognitive developmental tradition, leads to a more adaptive stance for future transitions.

Transformation from the Institutional Balance:

Most adults move out of an exploratory mode and make major career commitments at some point. In psychosocial terms, adults enter "establishment" and "maintenance" career phases (Super, 1957). Recent revisions of career phase theory point to a so-called mid-career reappraisal phenomenon, in which issues of boredom, obsolescence, and involuntary career change arise to challenge the person to make new career meanings. Institutionally based meaning-making, which in some ways can be regarded as a triumph during young adulthood, can be a deficit at this mid-career phase.

The challenge of adult career reappraisal can, under favorable conditions, trigger development in the direction of an interindividual perspective. In contrast to the example of the college student (who was helped to find and act on a stable center within herself), the overly individuated, institutionally balanced client should be encouraged to embrace newness and contradiction while still making commitments. From this more flexible interindividual perspective, the hard-won "project" (e.g., current career role) is open to question: "Do I get what I want out of these projects?" or, even more important, "Can I reexamine what it is that I really want?" The institutional-to-interindividual transformation is a shift from embeddedness in a current form to a consideration of the basic purposes of any forms (e.g., occupational) that the person might choose to take.

Institutionally embedded career decision-askers can be challenged to hear their own inner, contradictory voices and those of others who say, "You are more than this current job, profession, or belief system; these are but forms for bigger purposes and needs that may be expressed in many ways. Try to let a little light shine on the sealed-up system that you are now."

> Consider the case of Jim, age 40, who experienced a back injury that prevented him from continuing his work as a commercial fisherman. He concluded that his only alternative was to pursue his current occupation in which he had invested time and other resources. Jim felt that he had to maintain a commercial position, because, in his words, "Well, I've always been a commercial fisherman; I wouldn't know how to be anything but that!" Jim had identified his self with his current occupational form.

Using Loder's first moment (conscious conflict) as a guide, I helped Jim consider his conflict intentionally and consciously. One aspect of this conflict was that he wished to express the entrepreneurial side of himself, which had been submerged. Through a process of supporting him in his predicament, encouraging him to take time to reflect (Loder's second moment—pause), and challenging him to consider other forms and purposes in his life, Jim opted to get started in restaurant work. An image (Loder's third moment) had emerged, had been fleshed out (moment four, repatterning), and was consequently acted on (moment five, interpretation).

Such change might have been limited to job or occupational change, but Jim later said, "More than making this one change, I've reconsidered the entire way I make choices; whereas before I was locked into a kind of manual worker image of myself, I now feel freer to step into new roles. I can see multiple possibilities for myself in the future, if I can remain open to my experiences and recognize my changing needs; I just feel more open and determined." The seeds of the institutional to interindividual shift can be heard in Jim's words. The institutionally embedded adult can be helped by the developmentally oriented counselor to become more comfortable with incompleteness and, therefore, to consider unexplored, alternate expressions of the self.

DILEMMA HOLDING – AN ACTIVITY FOR
PROMOTING TRANSFORMATION

Kegan has developed a specific activity that can help adults develop more adaptively in mid-career: development is intentionally promoted by means of explicitly encouraging them to consider and even cherish contradictions in their work life. In this activity, clients are asked to reflect on what is dissonant for them in their careers. First, a conflict-highlighting question is posed: "How could your work be going better than it is now?" Next, participants reflect on, in order: (a) the beliefs or convictions that form the foundation to the responses to the question; (b) the competing, contradictory, hidden beliefs that maintain the status quo; and (c) their contributions to the less-than-optimal expression of the beliefs under the first reflection.

Through this activity, Kegan suggests, persons hold themselves "in jeopardy of learning," first by becoming aware of the contradictions and then by working to resolve the conflicts. Furthermore, Kegan has suggested that resolution occurs in a group, which provides a supportive context for working on challenges to one's equilibrium. He suggests that complete resolution of the conflict is not the goal; rather, increasing comfort in living with such tensions signals developmental growth. Thus, this activity may help clients regularly welcome dissonant information, in contrast to denial, to honestly face competing aspects of themselves, and to solve not merely a problem but to "solve themselves."

CONCLUSION

Career counseling can be construed as a development-enhancing activity – one that helps clients achieve greater flexibility, renew their self-definition, and live in a transformational, dialectical environment. The principles of constructive-developmental theory may serve as a foundation for a career counseling paradigm in which career is treated as a quest, an unfolding that requires active participation by the meaning-making client.

In this formulation, neo-Piagetian constructive developmental theory describes what effective counseling has always accomplished: encourage clients to transform limiting, dysfunctional conceptions of themselves into possibilities that reflect greater opportunities for self-expression, and become less limited by circumscribed roles and more responsive to fundamental needs and talents. While career counselors continue to help clients accumulate new information about themselves and their environments, they also must help clients identify their unarticulated fundamental values and needs, explore the competing beliefs that render those values unexpressed, and translate the implications of this exploration into viable actions that are authentic responses to the exploration.

From the constructive-developmental perspective, seemingly simple transitions can be opportunities for deep structural transformation. The counselor's tasks are to assess his or her clients' implicit meaning-making stances and challenge and support clients in their dilemmas in such a way that clients become open to new possibilities.

REFERENCES

Bar-Yam, M. (1991). Do women and men speak in different voices? *International Journal of Aging and Human Development, 32,* 247–259.

Basseches, M. (1984). *Dialectical thinking and adult development.* Norwood, NJ: Ablex.

Greenhaus, J. H. (1987). *Career management.* Chicago: Dryden Press.

Kegan, R. (1982). *The evolving self.* Cambridge, MA: Harvard University Press.

Loder, J. E. (1989). *The transforming moment.* Colorado Springs, CO: Helmers & Howard.

McAuliffe, G. J., & Neukrug, E. (1992, September). *Training the counselor to understand pluralism: The developmental perspective.* Paper presented at the meeting of the American Association for Counseling and Supervision, San Antonio, TX.

Piaget, J. (1970). *The principles of genetic epistemology.* London: Rutledge & Keegan.

Super, D. E. (1957). *The psychology of careers.* New York: Harper & Row.

2

Client Resistance to Career Counseling

Lewis E. Patterson, EdD

Dr. Patterson is Professor Emeritus of Counseling in the College of Education at Cleveland State University, Cleveland, OH.

KEY POINTS

- Many clients who seek help with career counseling ironically resist making decisions and examining certain events, relationships, and responsibilities.

- Any kind of change, even desired and sought-after change, can create anxiety. Many clients are too anxious to engage optimally in making career-related decisions. Career counselors should be experienced in helping clients with cognitive decision making.

- Fears that clients commonly experience during career counseling include: fear of making unfavorable discoveries about one's ability, fear of failing to satisfy significant others, fear of moving to new levels of responsibility, fear of giving up dependency on significant others for one's keep, fear of becoming trapped in an irrevocable course of action, and fear of giving up the comparative comfort of a known present for a more uncertain future.

- Clients often are not fully aware of their thoughts that sustain fear. The counseling process may include helping clients become more able to identify and articulate such fear-producing thoughts.

- Career counselors should never focus on decision making with an indecisive client who is resisting the entire counseling process. Rather, recognizing the client's fear can provide an opportunity for that fear to be expressed and elaborated.

- Counselors can help their clients confront fear by using the three-stage model of counseling outlined in this chapter.

RECOLLECTIONS

Remember, if you will, the last time you went through the process of changing jobs. If we place that transition in the most positive context, you may have been moving from a successful experience in a position that you had outgrown to seek a wider opportunity for the future. Even if this was your fortunate experience and you landed the new job you sought, what were your feelings during the time of the transition?

If you were typical, you probably felt excitement about the prospect of new challenges. But, most likely, you were anxious about whether your credentials presented you well enough, whether you would perform well in interviews, whether potential employers would recognize your talents, whether you would *really* like the new position if offered it, how you would react to rejection notices, whether you would miss the familiarity of your previous position, and whether your new manager would be supportive.

Pursuing your recollections further — back to an earlier time in your life — try to remember what it was like to make your first transition from dependence on your family to the advent of your life as an independent decision maker. For many of you, this major life change will have coincided with entering college and facing myriad questions, such as: what will I study, will that be best for me, where will I live, what if I don't succeed?

The point of this recollection exercise is to help you reexperience the anxieties of some of your own transitions. If one or more of your transitions involved dismissal, failure, or blocked goals, you will have had especially strong emotions about the experience — emotions much more like those of many clients who seek career counseling.

Clearly, career decisions (and educational decisions that lead to career outcomes) are not simple, unencumbered, rational experiences — even in the most predictable of circumstances. Counselors appropriately encourage their clients to use a variety of cognitive analysis skills to reach clearer understandings of personal attributes and career opportunities. But, for some clients, the anxieties surrounding choices impair cognitive processes and hinder the ability to act on decisions that may be reached.

RESISTANCE AS A RESPONSE TO FEAR OF CHANGE

Counselors have long recognized that many clients who seek help with life's concerns nevertheless resist the counselor's best efforts to encourage careful examination of certain events, relationships, and responsibilities. Such resistance is defined by Brammer, Shostrum, and Abrego (1989) as a characteristic of the client's defense system that opposes the purposes of counseling. In other words, even though the client has sought help, some aspect of the situation is so anxiety producing that the client still avoids fully encountering the experience.

Even though resistance opposes the purposes of self-understanding in counseling, it also helps the client avoid material that is just too painful to think about or discuss. Bugental and Bugental (1996) attribute resistance to the client's fear of changing his or her personal definition of self as well as how he or she construes the world.

Such resistance is expected and relatively easy to recognize when highly emotional personal problems such as marital discord, domestic violence, or mental illness are involved. But when the content of counseling is career related, it has often been assumed that clients can participate objectively and dispassionately in a decision-making process.

In the United States, our careers play a strong role in defining who we are. Because career decisions "affect one's future lifestyle, life space, economic promise, personal satisfaction, marital prospects — indeed the whole quality of life" (Patterson, 1993, p. 149), much is at stake. Career decisions can evoke a great deal of anxiety and lead a client who has requested help to avoid using the help, thereby resisting the process of exploration. Jordaan (1963) stated many years ago that "individuals guard against discoveries which cast doubt upon the self-picture" (p. 76).

SITUATIONS THAT ELICIT ANXIETY AND RESISTANCE

In the examples that follow, we examine some of the fears that clients commonly experience during career counseling and some of the personal thinking processes that sustain fear. The client often is not fully aware of this private thinking; part of the counseling process may include helping him or her become more able to articulate fear-producing thoughts.

Fear of Making Unfavorable Discoveries About One's Ability:

An example of the impact of this fear is a woman who contemplates reentering the world of work after a period of absence from the workforce devoted to raising a family. Many women in this circumstance believe that they have lost skills (including the ability to learn new skills) since they last worked. Furthermore, they often wrongfully assume that nothing they have done in managing a household and children has any relevance to being gainfully employed. They fear that they will be ineffective in the workplace and that if they get a job it will be only a matter of time until their incompetence is discovered.

Similar fears are attached to the idea of seeking further education or training. A woman who is carrying such negative thoughts may or may not choose to discuss them with a counselor. Either way, negative thinking often inhibits any steps that might move her closer to discovering her true potential.

Other examples of the fear that one will not be capable of adapting are seen in persons of both genders throughout the life span. We can think of the prevocational consequences of such fear in school-phobic kindergartners, and in executives who fear that their careers have plateaued and that they would fail at a new company.

Fear of Failing to Satisfy Significant Others:

A personal experience of mine might illustrate this kind of fear. I was born into a working-class family in which everyone was employed in occupations with a tangible outcome: carpenter, printer, electrician, machinist. However, my parents held the value that children should have the opportunity to achieve more than their parents, and it always had been taken for granted that I would attend college. I earned my first degree in the physical sciences (chemistry, physics, and geology — all disciplines whereby it was possible to see products of my efforts). Several years later, after having entered the counseling profession, I ran across the results of a Strong Interest Inventory that I had taken during my freshman orientation to college. I was astonished to see that my high interest scores were all in the behavioral sciences. I do not recall paying the slightest attention to the outcomes of my interest inventory. In retrospect, I believe that my resistance to receiving the information was directly related to a subliminal belief that my family would not have understood, and thus would not have approved of, work that would be devoted to "people skills" rather than to the creation of a product.

Fear of Moving to New Levels of Responsibility:

A familiar example of this kind of fear, sometimes called "senioritis," is observed in young people who seem paralyzed when faced with making choices as they finish high-school. They seem totally unable to address the choices they must make and avoid planning until the last possible moment. Such fear may resurface on graduation from college. Although the student often recognizes that society in general and parents in particular hold expectations of new levels of responsibility — either in a job or advanced education — he or she often denies the impending change and continues to act as though nothing is changing. Even when the student has been exposed to guidance activities that develop job-search and decision-making skills, resistance prevents him or her from acting on that knowledge.

Another important example of this kind of fear may be found in the older person who has progressed in a career but does not seek opportunities for more responsible roles. This may result in the failure to seek new employment when opportunities have been exhausted with the present employer, the failure to exhibit initiative in the present job, or the failure to seek appropriate promotions in the present environment. Often, the person does not even think about making any changes because the thoughts create anxiety.

Fear of Giving Up Dependency on Significant Others for One's Keep:

The fear of becoming independent is closely related to the fear of responsibility, as well as to the fear of not meeting the expectations of others. This type of resistance is often seen in clients who are in the process of making the transition to adulthood. The beginning worker may be accustomed to a standard of living sustainable by his or her mid-life parents. However, this level is not likely to be achieved initially by a beginning worker, and excessively high income expectations may set the client up for failure.

Fear of Becoming Trapped in an Irrevocable Course of Action:

The decision to pursue a certain career direction is in some ways similar to choosing a particular road when driving a car. For the time being, other courses of action are precluded. Given that career in our culture shapes the fabric of life, some people find the thought of passing up one option in order to pursue another one intolerably conflicting. This phenomenon may be most prevalent in multitalented persons who could legitimately succeed in various endeavors.

Fear of Giving Up the Comparative Comfort of a Known Present for a More Uncertain Future:

This fear summarizes all those listed above and returns us to our definition of resistance as fear of change.

SUPPORTING CHANGE

When one recognizes that many clients fail to work on their career concerns out of fear, the range of counseling strategies needed to promote change expands. One of the biggest mistakes made by career counselors is the tendency to maintain focus on cognitive exploration and decision making with indecisive clients who are resisting the entire counseling process. In contrast, a counselor who recognizes the client's fear will provide opportunity for that fear to be expressed and elaborated. The purpose of such a discussion is to make the client's fear of growing an acceptable topic for counseling. Getting to the roots of the client's fear and helping the client resolve or at least manage the fear are prerequisite to exploration and decision making.

Strategies that have long been recognized as important in personal counseling become paramount for the career counselor who is working with a resistant client. When used effectively, these strategies establish the client's readiness to engage in the decision-making process.

Confronting Fear Using a Three-Stage Model of Counseling:

Patterson and Welfel (1994) presented a three-stage model of the counseling process that can be used to encourage a client to face the fears that may preclude effective decision making.

Stage 1

In the first stage, the counselor encourages client self-disclosure through good attending skills and active listening. This is the *initial disclosure/relationship-building phase* of counseling, during which the counselor's undivided attention, genuineness, and empathic understanding make the client feel safe and valued as a person.

The following purposes are served during the initial disclosure stage of counseling:

- The client has an opportunity to describe what concerns brought him or her to counseling.

- The counselor learns of the client's background, personality, and coping skills.

- Through telling about self and concerns, the client often makes new connections and gains new insights into how to solve his or her own problem.

- As the client tells his or her story, the act of sharing the problem often reduces the feeling of concern. It has often been said that "a problem shared is a problem halved."

During this first phase of counseling, the counselor may encounter some resistance, but it is *rarely* productive to confront resistance *directly*. Instead, the counselor should paraphrase the client's statements and reflect the client's feelings, both to show understanding and to prompt the client's continued efforts at self-exploration.

Many career counselors tend to shortchange the initial disclosure stage of counseling. They tend to be solution oriented and often do not take the time to capture all the nuances of the client's situation before moving to the development of solutions. Unfortunately, a client who does not feel that he or she has been understood often has little faith that solutions generated in counseling will work. Resistance to implementing strategies for change will remain at a high level and progress will be slow.

Stage 2

The second stage of counseling is a time for *in-depth exploration*. By this time, the client has had time to begin to feel safe with the counselor and the counseling process, and, therefore, reveals more of his or her underlying motives and private thoughts. Sometimes, even the client is surprised by what he or she discovers in the process of deeper exploration. This is the time when, for example, a young man discovers that his feelings of dissatisfaction with his career really represent a feeling of rivalry with his spouse. Another client may discover that her repeated experiences with unreasonable supervisors represent a reaction to all authority figures rather than a series of unfortunate employment choices. This client often will then be able to talk about unresolved conflict with one or both parents. From your own experience, try to add to this list of examples of clients who were unable to make good decisions about their careers because they were not fully aware of what influenced their behaviors.

During the second stage of counseling, the counselor can address resistance a little more directly because the client is now feeling safer in discussing private matters. It is acceptable for the counselor to use *advanced-level empathy statements* that help the client state directly what has only been implied. With these types of statements, the counselor makes connections that the client has not yet seen. This must be done carefully and tentatively, because the client, you will remember, has used defenses to reduce anxiety. As the counselor asks the client to relinquish the defenses, the client's fears will rise — even though giving up the defense may be necessary for progress to be made.

Consider Robert, who was born with a congenitally malformed left hand that had no useful fingers but a thumb with oppositional strength against the palm of the hand. Robert also had difficulty with school and completed only the ninth grade, thus limiting the scope of his potential employment. At age 23, he had never held steady employment and was exploring with a counselor how he might gain training needed to be employable. An interest inventory had indicated preferences for occupations reflecting Holland's realistic and conventional codes. Although it was clear to the counselor that Robert had simply avoided making even tentative choices of occupation since leaving school, he encouraged Robert to look at various machine operation and retail merchandising options. The retailing options captured no interest; machine operation seemed to spark passing attention. But after brief consideration, Robert would dismiss each choice. The counselor finally said, "Robert, you really seem to be interested in jobs involving machinery, yet you cannot seem to picture yourself in such jobs. I wonder if you keep pulling back because you are not confident you could manage such work with your hand."

Although Robert was initially reluctant to discuss directly the use of his hand, this comment helped him realize that he was rejecting all occupations requiring use of his hands without considering whether he could perform the particular functions needed. With full use of his right hand and considerable facility with the oppositional thumb of the left, he came to realize that there were jobs he could manage. He eventually settled on training to operate road grading equipment and has now worked for 20 years in that line of work. The advanced-level empathy statement reflected what Robert's behavior indicated about his thought processes, even though Robert himself was not fully aware of how he was thinking.

Interpretation is an extremely useful technique in the second stage of Patterson and Welfel's model. Through interpretation, the counselor helps the client understand his or her behavior by offering possible explanations for the behavior based on psychological principles or clinical experience. Consider the client who works for unreasonable supervisors. The counselor can say something like, "Sometimes when a person has had conflicts with an important person such as a parent, he or she tends to feel controlled by other persons who remind him or her of that person. Do you suppose this could be happening to you?"

Another counseling task in the second stage is to help the client see discrepancies in his or her remarks and actions. For example, consider the case of a client who laments the fact that she has not been promoted but who discloses that she misses work often and is late on the average of three times a month. A constructive confrontation might be, "Help me to understand. You are trying to impress your supervisors that you can handle more responsibility, yet you aren't very punctual or regular about your work hours." In making such a confrontation, it is important to keep the tone supportive and caring rather than critical. The client needs to know you are on her side, even when pointing to discrepancies.

Stage 3

Patterson and Welfel refer to the third stage of counseling as a *commitment to action*. This is the stage of counseling in which it becomes possible to generate alternative courses of action and choose among them. Once choices are made, the client tries to implement the choices and continues to receive coaching and support from the counselor. The emotional overlay that prevented effective cognitive decision making is now under control and the client's coping skills are at a higher level. The typical career counseling process of trying to match personal qualities and motives with opportunities is now much more feasible.

Even in this third stage of counseling, however, we cannot assume resistance is nonexistent. After all, this is the time when the client is actually encouraged to implement change, and the action may still cause apprehension. For example, a client may state that he or she wants to continue schooling, but does not act when supplied with information about how to select and apply for the training. To help the client act on her own behalf, the counselor might say "Theresa, please help me understand. You have said that you want to go back to school, but it is 3 weeks since I gave you some leads to follow — and it seems that you have not taken any action." This will expose the resistance and help both counselor and client determine what needs to transpire next. It may be that more specific steps to implement the plan are required, or that the decision to return to school was not explored thoroughly enough and should be examined further.

As a final note on supporting change, it is important to recognize that different clients require different amounts of time to progress through the three stages. All three stages *may* occur in a single session; however, with more complicated circumstances and higher anxiety levels, several sessions may be needed. Sometimes, rehearsing the action steps will increase client understanding of what must be done and will encourage the client to commit to a course of action.

THE CASE OF DANIEL

Daniel arrived at the university counseling center in a state of considerable agitation. He was a 19-year-old sophomore enrolled in a pre-medical curriculum. His presenting problem was that he had just received his grades for the previous semester and had failed chemistry, a required course in his pre-med program.

In the privacy of the counselor's office, Dan began crying as he described that his life was over. He explained that he was the only son in a family where both his father and grandfather were medical doctors. According to Dan, his had assumed since the time of his birth that he, too, would become a physician. Dan had internalized this expectation so completely that he had never considered any other career option. He had just failed chemistry, and, in his view, had failed himself and his family.

Typical of many clients in crisis, Daniel was processing information very poorly. He had quickly concluded that his failing the chemistry course would result in his being dropped from the pre-med program and that he could never become a doctor. Gentle efforts by the counselor to question whether this was an accurate picture of the consequences were met with resistance. At first, Daniel said that it did not matter whether the department would dismiss him: he had disgraced himself and his family and he could not continue. Temporarily pursuing another line of thought, the counselor asked Daniel to consider what he would do next, assuming that he might be dropped from the program. He could not think of anything else that he was interested in doing and responded that the only thing he could think of was suicide. Accordingly, the counselor assessed Daniel's risk of committing suicide and concluded that no serious plan existed.

In time, Daniel's cathartic experience of sharing his deep fear with the counselor began to have a calming effect, and he stopped crying. The question of what action the pre-med department would take was revisited, and Daniel agreed that it made sense for him to discuss the options with his advisor. The counselor encouraged Daniel to call for an appointment before leaving the office. Another appointment was made with the counselor for the next day after the scheduled time with the advisor, and Daniel was given an emergency number to call if he found himself feeling suicidal before the next contact.

When Daniel arrived for the next session, he was considerably calmer and reported that his meeting with his advisor had gone well. He would be permitted to repeat the chemistry course, but the first grade would also remain on his transcript. Also, because of the sequencing of courses, his progress through the program would be delayed by a semester.

Knowing that this option existed seemed to free Daniel to approach his dilemma further with less anxiety. As the counselor accepted Daniel's anxiety, the client was able to say that he did not like chemistry and was not certain that he really wanted to repeat it. Furthermore, he had come to view the *work* leading up to becoming a doctor and *being* a doctor as two entirely separate things. He had always seen the status and lifestyle of his father and grandfather as desirable, but he was beginning to realize that he really did not like the science that formed the core of the work. This was a frightening thought because it led to the conclusion that he might need to make a different career choice for which he was not prepared and of which, he believed, his family would disapprove.

The counselor began working with Daniel's concern about making another choice. Daniel was given plenty of room to mull over his anxiety — that he could not make another choice — and his feeling of loss about a plan that he had harbored since childhood. Discussion then moved to those things about a physician's life that Daniel had always considered desirable. The key elements were the prestige of a position of importance, work that centered on the manipulation of ideas rather than objects, the opportunity for personal contact with patients, and the chance to be of service to others. Although the counselor made immediate connections to a variety of human services careers, he terminated the session by helping Daniel record these criteria on paper, with the instruction that Daniel should try to add to the list and to think of occupations that might fit the criteria. The counselor hoped that Daniel was now feeling less resistant and that his cognitive skills might lead him to some discoveries about new possibilities.

At the beginning of the next session, Daniel indicated that he did not really have other criteria to add and that the only alternative career he had thought of was law — not a particularly exciting option to him. Discussion led to the conclusion that while a law career met all his criteria, the content of the legal code held absolutely no fascination for him. Exploration then turned to college courses that had piqued his interest. He had enjoyed and performed well in English composition, American literature, and psychology. He had especially enjoyed writing a short story about a summer adventure and found connections between the ideas from his psychology course and the characters in the literature. The counselor now felt that Daniel's resistance to considering a career in human services would be low enough to ask if he had ever thought about being a psychologist or a counselor. Daniel gradually began to warm to this possibility, with his major concern revolving around the probability that his family would object.

Next steps in the counseling process involved the provision of career information about psychology and related careers. Daniel thought the work sounded interesting, but the prestige factor remained a hindrance. The counselor acknowledged that medical careers were among the most highly respected in ratings of prestige and allowed time for Daniel to process this. Finally, Daniel concluded that the work of a psychologist would be important work to him, even if not so highly valued by others.

The final step involved planning and rehearsing how Daniel would present his situation and his new plan to his family. He fully expected his parents to express disappointment and even anger. The counselor role-played some scenes with Daniel so that he could learn how to express his needs despite the anger that might be expressed by members of his family.

The final stage of dealing with the client's resistance entailed helping him to understand the phases of growth he had experienced so that he could help his parents follow that same process, thereby removing the final obstacle to making a decision. Daniel later expressed surprise and pleasure that, although disappointed and initially angry, his parents had ultimately been able to reaffirm their love for him and their support for his need to define his own life.

A careful review of this case study will reveal that the counselor was well aware of Daniel's resistance. In the earliest stage of counseling, the counselor allowed much opportunity for Daniel to introduce his crisis situation, his history, and his feelings of self-doubt. Deeper exploration as time passed allowed the client to begin to separate himself from his own previous view of self and from perceived family expectations. Only when these two steps had led to a new readiness was it possible for Daniel to use his cognitive decision-making skills to arrive at a new plan.

CONCLUSION

Career counselors tend to be experienced in the process of helping clients with cognitive decision making. This chapter has presented the position that many clients are too anxious to engage optimally in making decisions. Beginning with the proposition that any kind of change—even desired and sought-after change—can create anxiety, we have examined several sources of anxiety related to career growth. People fear that they will not be successful in new endeavors, that others will not approve, that they will have to be responsible in new ways, and that they will become trapped into living with bad decisions.

Career counselors who learn to place more emphasis on the first two stages of counseling (initial disclosure and in-depth exploration) will enable their clients to engage more effectively in decision making. Although it is never possible for a counselor to remove the fear associated with change (actually change in self), it is possible to help clients overcome their resistance and act more effectively to accomplish their goals.

REFERENCES

Brammer, L. M., Shostrum, E. L., & Abrego, P. J. (1989). *Therapeutic psychology* (5th ed.). Englewood Cliffs, NJ: Prentice-Hall.

Bugental, J. F. T., & Bugental, E. K. (1996). Resistance to and fear of change. In *The Hatherleigh guide to psychotherapy* (pp. 33-46). New York: Hatherleigh Press.

Jordaan, J. P. (1963). Exploratory behavior: the formation of self and occupational concepts. In D. E. Super (Ed.), *Career development: Self-concept theory.* CEEB Research Monograph, 4, pp. 42-78.

Patterson, L. E. (1993). Resistance as a factor in career counseling. *Journal of Career Development, 19,* 149-159.

Patterson, L. E., & Welfel, E. R. (1994). *The counseling process* (4th ed.). Pacific Grove, CA: Brooks/Cole.

FOR FURTHER READING

Brown, D., & Brooks, L. (1991). *Career counseling techniques.* Boston: Allyn & Bacon.

Clark, A. J. (1990). The identification and modification of defense mechanisms in counseling. *Journal of Counseling and Development, 69,* 231–236.

Dyer, W. W., & Vriend, J. (1975). *Counseling techniques that work.* Washington, DC: APGA Press.

Gysbers, N. C., & Moore, E. J. (1987). *Career counseling: Techniques for practitioners.* Englewood Cliffs, NJ: Prentice-Hall.

Kaplan, D. M., & Brown, D. (1987). The role of anxiety in career indecisiveness. *Career Development Quarterly, 36,* 148-169.

Salomone, P. R. (1982). Difficult cases in career counseling, II: The indecisive client. *Personnel and Guidance Journal, 60,* 496-500.

3

Vocational Assessment and the ADA: Issues and Approaches for the Rehabilitation Professional

Stephen W. Thomas, EdD, CVE, CRC

Dr. Thomas is Professor and Director, Graduate Program in Vocational Evaluation, Department of Rehabilitation Studies, East Carolina University, Greenville, NC.

KEY POINTS

- The Americans with Disabilities Act (ADA) promotes the rights of persons with disabilities in five areas: employment, transportation, public accommodations, state and local government, and telecommunications. This chapter discusses Title I, employment, which provides equal employment opportunities based on merit rather than quotas.

- The key to a successful ADA-based vocational evaluation or assessment is the accurate identification of functional strengths and limitations and the determination of reasonable accommodations that can minimize or eliminate limitations.

- Regulations used to establish the qualifications of persons with disabilities cover two areas: (a) diagnosis and (b) assessment and evaluation. Diagnosis must be established before a vocational assessment is initiated. Vocational assessment is used to determine whether the client fits the other two requirements for the disability definition: "substantial limitation" and "major life activities."

- The ADA provides guidelines for the identification and use of standardized instruments for employment screening purposes. These guidelines should be uniformly applied in evaluations.

INTRODUCTION

The Americans with Disabilities Act (ADA) is designed to promote and enhance the rights of persons with disabilities with respect to five areas: employment, transportation, public accommodations, state and local government, and telecommunications. Title I provides for equal employment opportunities for persons with disabilities based on merit rather than quotas. This appropriate focus on merit requires that rehabilitation professionals work closely with their clients to prepare them for the demands of the jobs they desire. However, the ADA is more than a law — it is a commitment to ensuring that qualified individuals with disabilities are "given the same consideration for employment that individuals without disabilities are given" (ADA, 1991).

This chapter will focus on Title I: employment, as it relates to (a) diagnosis of disability and (b) vocational evaluation and assessment of persons with disabilities. It will interpret those sections of the ADA that are pertinent to vocational assessment and will suggest practical approaches to implementing appropriate evaluation strategies.

Because the ADA was passed relatively recently, sufficient case law is not available to provide a definitive interpretation. However, case law from Section 504 of the Rehabilitation Act of 1973 can be used until the ADA has developed its own history. The ideas presented in this chapter are no more than suggestions and have been untested with regard to the ADA provisions. If a reasonable effort is made to administer the recommended procedures fairly and objectively, the rehabilitation professional may be viewed as acting in good faith.

Regulations to establish the qualifications of individuals with disabilities cover two distinct areas:

1. *Diagnosis:* to establish the existence of a physical or mental impairment that significantly limits major life activities

2. *Assessment and evaluation*: to determine the functional strengths and limitations of the individual with a disability and to identify reasonable accommodations to overcome the specified functional limitations

Within the rehabilitation process, diagnosis and verification of the impairment must be accomplished before a vocational assessment is initiated. It is determined by a specialist (e.g., physician, psychologist) who is qualified to diagnose a physical or mental impairment. Conditions covered under the ADA are:

- Any physiologic disorder, or condition, cosmetic disfigurement, or anatomic loss affecting one or more of the following body systems: neurologic, musculoskeletal, special sense organs, respiratory (including speech organs), cardiovascular, reproductive, digestive, genitourinary, hemic and lymphatic, skin and endocrine

- Any mental or psychological disorder, such as mental retardation, organic brain syndrome, emotional or mental illness, and specific learning disabilities (ADA, 1991, p. 35735).

Once diagnosis has established the existence of a physical or mental impairment, the impact of that disability on functioning levels can be assessed by a rehabilitation professional (e.g., rehabilitation counselor, vocational evaluator, rehabilitation specialist) either informally or formally.

ASSESSMENT

The informal procedure, often called *vocational assessment*, involves the use of techniques such as file review, interviewing, functional assessment, and the administration of a few standardized tests (e.g., interest, achievement, dexterity).

The formal procedure, referred to as *vocational evaluation,* goes beyond the use of simple vocational assessment techniques to incorporate more comprehensive and formalized procedures such as extensive standardized testing, work sample administration, behavior observation, situational assessment, and on-the-job evaluation. Usually conducted by a qualified vocational evaluator, this process is used when an informal assessment fails to yield sufficient information. Vocational evaluations generally conclude with a report that details results and recommendations.

Although the diagnostic process can also identify functional levels, rehabilitation practitioners are able to use various assessment and evaluation techniques to profile the types and degrees of functional strengths and limitations. Assessment can be effectively used to address the last two parts of the disability definition—"substantially limits" and "major life activities."

The second critical element in the definition, "major life activities," means

> functions such as caring for oneself, performing manual tasks, walking, seeing, hearing, speaking, breathing, learning, and working. (ADA, 1991, p. 35735)

The interpretive section of the ADA in the *Federal Register* indicates that this is not an "exhaustive" list—it may also include other activities such as "sitting, standing, lifting, reaching" (ADA, 1991, p. 35735).

FUNCTIONAL ASSESSMENT

"Functions" is a key word used to describe major life activities that has been well defined and used within the field of rehabilitation (Crewe & Athelstan, 1984; Halpern & Fuhrer, 1984; Moon, Goodall, Barcus, & Brooke, 1986; Tenth Institute on Rehabilitation Issues, 1983). Numerous inventories are commercially available, and many practitioners have modified existing forms or developed their own for specialized applications. Following are two definitions of functional assessment that relate to the requirements of the ADA:

> In simplest terms, functional assessment is a systematic enumeration of vocationally relevant strengths and limitations. (Crewe & Athlestan, 1984, p. 3)

This first definition refers specifically to "relevant strengths and limitations," which become critically important when considering other ADA terms such as "substantially limits," "essential functions," and "reasonable accommodation." As indicated in the definition, functional assessment should allow for the "systematic" review of all functional areas listed on an inventory. Although this definition focuses on the phrase "vocationally relevant," most functional assessment forms are more broadly used and interpreted with regard to community functioning.

Given this need for more flexible utility, a second definition also has application to the ADA:

> Functional assessment is the measurement of purposeful behavior in interaction with the environment, which is interpreted according to the assessment's intended uses. (Halpern & Fuhrer, 1984, p. 3)

This definition emphasizes the importance of environment and its influence on behavior and is not specific to any one setting or purpose. It speaks to the diversity of information often sought through the administration of functional assessment procedures.

Most functional assessment forms are well suited to identifying those functional aspects associated with "major life activities" (e.g., vision, hearing, memory, endurance, motor speed, perception, learning ability). These forms provide opportunities for rating functioning in a wide range of work and nonwork activities using descriptive appraisals rather than discrete or continuous rating scales such as above average/ average/below average or good/fair/poor. For example, rather than using a Likert-type scale to rate mathematical ability (from a 5 for above average to 1 for below average), functional statements can be substituted, such as:

5. Can use calculus and statistics

4. Can use algebra and geometry

3. Can do basic math with decimals and fractions

2. Can do basic math with whole numbers

1. Can count to 200

Some forms were designed to be used with a general rehabilitation population (Crewe & Athelstan, 1984), and others were created to assess individuals with severe disabilities (Moon et al., 1986). Most inventories must be completed by rehabilitation practitioners, but others can be completed by clients or their family members (Crewe & Athelstan, 1984). Some companion forms are even designed for use as a functional job analysis inventory to enhance the job accommodation and job match process (Moon et al., 1986). Because these are simply data collection forms, they can be completed during file review, interviewing, observation, testing, vocational evaluation, situational assessment, and staffing processes in a variety of settings (e.g., work, school, home, community, recreation). They do not dictate how information should be collected as long as it is current and accurate.

Functional assessment is not without its problems. There is a lack of uniformity and standardization among forms, assessment strategies, and recording procedures, resulting in questionable reliability and validity. However, as long as the process remains systematic, broad based, and descriptive, it should be a useful tool for the initial development of a functional profile of strengths and limitations. The information collected can then be used to develop a plan for evaluating the extent and nature of the identified functional limitations and beneficial accommodations.

DETERMINING SUBSTANTIAL LIMITATION

The ADA requires that the degree of the functional limitation be established. Only when there is a "substantial limitation" will this third and final critical element in the disability definition be met. In the ADA, the term "substantially limits" means:

- Unable to perform a major life activity that the average person in the general population can perform

- Significantly restricted as to the condition, manner or duration under which an individual can perform a particular major life activity as compared to the condition, manner, or duration under which the average person in the general population can perform that same major life activity (ADA, 1991, p. 35735).

Because "substantially limits" lacks a descriptive or quantifiable definition, professionals will need to rely on guidelines available from other sources. Two elements are important to making the definition of "substantially limits" operational: "significantly" and "average person in the general population."

The phrase "average person in the general population" suggests the type of norm group that should be used with tests and work samples. The interpretive section of the Act specifically states that the "average person is not intended to imply a precise mathematical average" (ADA, 1991). Therefore, other measurement principles will need to be considered.

"Significant," however, is a word that does carry a certain statistical inference. Within the field of standardized testing, standard deviation (SD) has been used as a tool to interpret, classify, and diagnose; it often represents scores that "significantly" deviate from the "mathematical average" (or mean).

When interpreting the Wechsler Adult Intelligence Scale-Revised, a 15-point (1 SD) or greater difference has been used to describe "significant" differences in scores or scores that are considered diagnostically "significant" (Anastasi, 1988; Drummond, 1988; Matarazzo, 1972; Wechsler, 1970).

An additional use of standard deviation as a classification tool can be found in the fourth edition of the *Diagnostic and Statistical Manual of Mental Disorders* (DSM-IV) (American Psychiatric Association [APA], 1994), in which the diagnostic criteria for mental retardation are defined by IQ ranges beginning at the scores and standard deviation levels indicated in Table 3.1. Although Borderline Intellectual Functioning (IQ beginning around 84, -1 SD) is covered in this section of the DSM-IV, it is not considered to be mental retardation.

Specific learning disabilities and neurological impairments have also used standard deviation differences in various test scores as a method of identifying the degree of impairment (Smith, 1988; Vocational Rehabilitation Center of Allegheny County, 1983). For example, the Symbol Digit Modalities Test of cerebral dysfunction lists standard deviations in the norm table for scoring purposes (Smith, 1988). The manual states that Low Scores fall at approximately 1 SD below the mean, Moderately Low Scores at 1.5 SD below the mean, and Very Low Scores at 2 SD below the mean. Although the author of that test considers scores at -1.5 SD for a normal group of adults to be the cutoff score for dysfunction, other research studies cited in the manual feel that scores in the -1 to -1.5 SD range "should be considered *suggestive* of cerebral dysfunction" (Smith, 1988, p. 6).

Table 3.1 DSM-IV DIAGNOSTIC CRITERIA FOR MENTAL RETARDATION		
Degree of Retardation	**Approx. IQ***	**Approx. SD**
Mild	55–70	-2
Moderate	40–55	-3
Severe	25–40	-4

* Does not include the measurement error of approximately five points.

Source: American Psychiatric Association. (1994). *Diagnostic and statistical manual of mental disorders* (4th ed.). Washington, DC: Author. Reprinted with permission from the American Psychiatric Association.

Using standard deviation as a means of determining the significance of a substantial limitation can be very useful. It also helps to achieve greater accuracy and consistency across groups when used in conjunction with other assessment strategies (e.g., functional assessment, observation, job analysis).

Applying the standard deviation technique requires close adherence to the following considerations:

- Care should be taken to choose tests and work samples that have content similar to the variety of functions associated with major life activities.

- Tests and work samples should have general population and employed-worker norms. Disability norms should be avoided because they may not reflect the general population.

- Standard deviation scores, as opposed to mean scores (50th percentile), should be used as one mechanism for determining which major life activities have significant, substantial limitations.

Table 3.2 is a proposed guideline for determining the significance of a substantial limitation. These guidelines may prove useful except when other recognized federal standards are available. For example, the National Institute of Education, Department of Education, has defined functional illiteracy as reading (words and comprehension), arithmetic, and spelling below a 4.9 grade level (Vocational Rehabilitation Center of Allegheny County, 1983). This may serve as a more acceptable guideline when determining substantial limitation in regard to the general population. On the other hand, grade levels above 4.9 in some clients may be considered limiting when technical and professional jobs requiring high academic

| **Table 3.2** | | | |
| **DETERMINING THE SIGNIFICANCE OF A LIMITED FUNCTION** | | | |
SD	Approx. percentile	Degree of limitation	Goals of Assessment
-1	16th	could be significant	Ascertain function's significance to essential life or work functions. Determine if accommodation is required.
-2	2nd	significant	Verify limitation's impact on situation-specific functioning. Explore potential benefits of accommodations
-3	>1st	severe	Identify reasonable accommodations and appropriate rehabilitation services to minimize or overcome the limitation

achievement skills are being considered. Research needs to be conducted on the use of functional assessment forms/inventories, standard deviation cut-offs, and recognized federal guidelines as viable techniques for determining substantial limitations to major life activities.

The ADA also identifies additional factors to be considered when assessing substantial limitations to major life activities. These include:

- The nature and severity of the impairment

- The duration or expected duration of the impairment

- The permanent or long-term impact or the expected permanent or long-term impact resulting from the impairment (ADA, 1991, p. 35735)

The standard deviation method could be used to assess "severity of the impairment" along with a content-based comparison of the individual's current functioning to the demands of work and other life activities. The greater the discrepancy, the higher the chances of the impairment being severe. "Duration" of the impairment may best be determined through the diagnostic phase as well as by evaluating the "permanent or long-term impact" of the impairment.

THE MAJOR LIFE ACTIVITY OF WORKING

One of the many functions listed under "major life activities" is working. The ADA states that "with respect to the major life activity of working":

(1) The term "substantially limits" means significantly restricted in the ability to perform either a class of jobs or a broad range of jobs in various classes as compared to the average person having comparable training, skills and abilities. The inability to perform

a single particular job does not constitute a substantial limitation in the major life activity of working.

(2) The following factors may be considered in determining whether an individual is substantially limited in the major life activity of "working":

(A) The geographical area to which the individual has reasonable access;

(B) The job from which the individual has been disqualified because of an impairment, and the number and types of jobs utilizing similar training, knowledge, skills or abilities, within that geographical area, from which the individual is also disqualified because of the impairment (class of jobs); and/or

(C) The job from which the individual has been disqualified because of an impairment, and the number and types of other jobs not utilizing similar training, knowledge, skills or abilities, within that geographical area, from which the individual is also disqualified because of an impairment (broad range of jobs in various classes). (ADA, 1991, p. 35735)

The ability of the rehabilitation professional to conduct a transferable work skills assessment will be invaluable in meeting the requirements of this part of the ADA (Havranek et al., 1994). Occupational information resources such as the *Dictionary of Occupational Titles* (U.S. Department of Labor, 1991), the *Revised Classification of Jobs* (Field & Field, 1992), and computerized job search systems (Botterbusch, 1986) will be essential tools for this phase of the assessment. Because the ADA requires that individuals have reasonable access to jobs within their geographical area, labor market surveys and job banks representing local employment opportunities should be developed and regularly updated. Knowledge of job families, occupational categories, and job/occupational clusters provide the working knowledge for determining if a person with a disability can perform the duties of "a class of jobs or a broad range of jobs."

For the disabled individual to be covered under the ADA, the rehabilitation professional must be able to demonstrate exclusion from a broad range of jobs (Adams, 1991). For example, if a worker is unable to perform heavy lifting in a particular job setting (due to the unique arrangement of the work area) but is not restricted in others, this would not constitute a substantial limitation. However, if the worker is restricted from performing all jobs requiring heavy lifting regardless of setting, this would constitute a substantial limitation to that class of jobs.

Employed worker norm groups or predetermined time standards (e.g., industrially generated performance standards such as Methods Time Measurement [MTM] and Modular Arrangement of Predetermined Time Systems [MODAPTS]) will need to be used with tests and work samples when determining substantial limitation. Interviewing, functional assessment, job analysis, situational assessment, and the standard deviation technique (as applied to tests and work samples) are useful evaluation tools when examining the major life activities of "working." Thorough knowledge of the labor market will result both in better accuracy in identifying substantial limitations to working and in suggestions for appropriate accommodations.

ASSESSING THE QUALIFIED INDIVIDUAL WITH A DISABILITY

It is important to understand what is meant by a "qualified individual with a disability." The ADA defines this as:

An individual with a disability who satisfies the requisite skill, experience, education and other job-related requirements of the employment position such individual holds or desires, and who, with or without reasonable accommodation, can perform the essential functions of such a position. (ADA, 1991, p. 35735)

The noteworthy components of this definition requiring closer examination include "reasonable accommodation" and "essential functions of such position." "Essential functions" means:

the fundamental job duties of the employment position the individual with a disability holds or desires. The term "essential functions" does not include the marginal functions of a position. (ADA, 1991, p. 35735)

A job function may be considered essential for any of several reasons, including but not limited to the following:

- The function may be essential because the reason the position exists is to perform that function

- The function may be essential because of the limited number of employees available among whom the performance of that job function can be distributed

- The function may be highly specialized so that the incumbent in the position is hired for his or her expertise or ability to perform the particular function (ADA, 1991, p. 35735)

Evidence of whether a particular function is essential includes, but is not limited to:

- The employer's judgment as to which functions are essential

- Written job descriptions prepared before advertising or interviewing applicants for the job

- The amount of time spent on the job performing the function

- The consequences of not requiring the incumbent to perform the function

- The term of a collective bargaining agreement

- The work experience of past incumbents in the job

- The current work experience of incumbents in similar jobs (ADA, 1991, p. 35735)

Initially, an ADA-based assessment process should be geared to examining the client holistically (i.e., developing an overall individual profile of functional strengths, limitations, and reasonable accommodation options). At that point, ecological issues (i.e., education, work, living, recreation, transportation, or personal/social/family) can be evaluated and environments matched to the individual's holistic profile.

"Essential functions" may only be important to the assessment process when a job match is being considered and when a detailed job analysis is available on the position in question. Assessment specialists involved in job analysis will need to have a thorough understanding of the process for determining essential functions. However, in cases where the evaluator is only responsible for conducting an assessment, other rehabilitation professionals responsible for job analysis will need to be provided with information sufficient to match client abilities with essential functions.

Several factors in the above definition are worth exploring. First, one of the best "litmus tests" of an essential function may be found in the statement, "The consequences of not requiring the incumbent to perform the function. . ." If the job cannot be successfully completed by a worker without performing the function, with or without reasonable accommodation, then the function would be considered essential.

The second important factor relates to phrases such as "reason position exists," "function may be highly specialized," and "amount of time spent on the job performing the function." A comprehensive job analysis focuses on four primary criteria: (a) a description of the duties of the job, (b) an evaluation of the difficulty level of the duties, (c) a consideration of the physical or environmental setting, and (d) a rating of the importance of each duty.

When considered with other ADA regulations (e.g., amount of time spent performing that function), three criteria stand out as highly useful when analyzing essential job functions:

1. The most difficult task(s)

2. The most important task(s)

3. The most time-consuming task(s)

Counselors and evaluators can provide employers with invaluable assistance on how to determine what job functions are essential as well as methods of incorporating this information into current job descriptions (Peterson, 1991). Rehabilitation professionals must be sensitive to the fact that job descriptions may not always contain current duties and activities because employers generally concentrate their efforts more on finding ways to improve overall performance rather than on updating descriptions that reflect the new demands.

The second important part of the definition for "qualified individual with a disability" is that of "reasonable accommodation." Under the ADA, "reasonable accommodation" means:

- Modifications or adjustments to a job application process that enable a qualified applicant with a disability to be considered for the position such qualified applicant desires

- Modifications or adjustments to the work environment, or to the manner or circumstances under which the position held or desired is customarily performed, that enable a qualified individual with a disability to perform the essential functions of that position

- Modifications or adjustments that enable a covered entity's employee with a disability to enjoy equal benefits and privileges of employment as are enjoyed by its other similarly situated employees without disabilities (ADA, 1991, pp. 35735–35736)

Vocational assessment plays an important role in evaluating the three major facets of "reasonable accommodation": job-seeking skills, job performance skills, and equal access to employment benefits and privileges. Through the use of information questionnaires and interviews (such as sample job application forms), the specialist can determine if the client, with or without modifications or adjustments, can successfully apply and interview for a job. Holistic and ecological assessments can be used to evaluate the performance and environmental aspects of the job and the need for accommodations.

In light of this new legislation, rehabilitation professionals must develop techniques for evaluating modifications needed by a client to access equal benefits and privileges of employment (e.g., full plant access, health insurance, recreation and leisure, educational opportunities). More generalized assessment strategies such as file review and interviewing can be used here until more valid procedures are available. In addition, Farley, Little, Bolton, and Chunn (N.D.) describe three work-related competencies (choosing a job, getting a job, keeping a job) that provide suggestions for evaluating the job application process and how the position is customarily performed.

With regard to actual job modifications for specific work tasks, "reasonable accommodation" may include:

- Making existing facilities used by employees readily accessible to and usable by individuals with disabilities

- Job restructuring; part-time or modified work schedules; reassignment to a vacant position; acquisition or modifications of equipment or devices; appropriate adjustment or modifications of examinations, training materials, or policies; the provision of qualified readers or interpreters; and other similar accommodations for individuals with disabilities (ADA, 1991, p. 35736)

By no means is this an exhaustive list, and it should be used to stimulate exploration into other types of accommodations. Rehabilitation engineering and assistive technology resources should be accessed on a case-by-case basis to help choose appropriate accommodations. It is important that potential accommodations be detailed in the vocational evaluation report so that all contingencies for successful placement can be included in the rehabilitation and placement plan.

Given the almost daily advances in assistive technology, most counselors and evaluators will be hard pressed to stay abreast of new developments. However, by establishing close working relationships with local rehabilitation engineers and learning to use national assistive technology data bases such as the Job Accommodation Network (JAN, telephone 1-800-526-7234), counselors and evaluators can gain greater insight in how best to solve accommodation problems. A unique aspect of vocational evaluation is the ability to try out modifications to determine how they affect performance. This serves as an opportunity to explore and identify accommodations that prove beneficial in evaluation and, therefore, may prove equally beneficial in the classroom or job site.

The ADA does not place all of the burden on the employer to determine which accommodation(s) would work best. It spells out a process whereby an employer can discuss accommodation needs with the prospective employee. The regulations state:

> To determine the appropriate reasonable accommodation it may be necessary for the covered entity to initiate an informal, interactive process with the qualified individual with a disability in need of the accommodation. The process should identify the precise limitations resulting from the disability and potential reasonable accommodations that could overcome those limitations. (ADA, 1991, p. 35736)

Throughout the assessment process, the specialist must routinely share results with clients and determine if they possess sufficient decision-making skills to understand and verbalize the results clearly. Only when we enlighten and empower our clients with assessment information can they become fully participating members of the rehabilitation team and independent job seekers.

One of the most beneficial skills we can teach our clients is how to explain to employers how they would go about performing specific job tasks and what reasonable accommodations would prove beneficial to ensuring competitive employment. Clients who are able to articulate approaches to — and accommodations for — specific work tasks will not require as much assistance in the placement process as individuals who are unable to understand or explain their employment strengths and needs. In that situation, someone would need to be empowered to speak on behalf of the client.

This process of empowerment involves sharing functional strengths and limitations profiles with clients and discussing their understanding of and agreement with their profiles. As accommodations are explored, clients can be asked if they know of beneficial modifications that can also be tried. All too often, rehabilitation practitioners make decisions concerning clients without really asking how they feel or what they can do.

Accommodations of essential functions may go beyond the

need to improve performance; some focus on the necessity to minimize dangers at the job site. The ADA refers to this as "direct threat," which is defined as:

a significant risk of substantial harm to the health or safety of the individual or others that cannot be eliminated or reduced by reasonable accommodation. The determination that an individual poses a "direct threat" shall be based on an individualized assessment of the individual's present ability to safely perform the essential functions of the job. This assessment shall be based on a reasonable medical judgment that relies on the most current medical knowledge and/or on the best available objective evidence. In determining whether an individual would pose a direct threat, the factors to be considered include:

(1) The duration of the risk;

(2) The nature and severity of the potential harm;

(3) The likelihood that the potential harm will occur;

(4) The imminence of the potential harm (ADA, 1991, p. 35736)

Knowledge of the job will improve the ability to target appropriate accommodations that will reduce or eliminate the specific threat and allow the worker to "safely perform the essential functions of the job." Without a detailed job and environmental analysis that includes potential job risks, the assessment can only make inferences about direct threat issues based on the known disability.

PROPER SELECTION AND USE OF EVALUATION INSTRUMENTS

The ADA provides specific guidelines for the identification

and use of standardized instruments for employment screening purposes. These guidelines should be uniformly applied in any appropriately administered evaluation. The first test-related regulation, "Qualification standards, tests, and other selection criteria," reads as follows:

> It is unlawful for a covered entity to use qualification standards, employment tests or other selection criteria that screen out or tend to screen out an individual with a disability or a class of individuals with disabilities, on the basis of disability, unless the standard, test or other selection criteria, as used by the covered entity, is shown to be job-related for the position in question and is consistent with business necessity. (ADA, 1991, p. 35737)

Counselors and evaluators should avoid using instruments and techniques that serve to screen clients out of jobs and services. Good evaluation practice is consistent with ADA regulations in that modifications and accommodations are routinely applied throughout the process and described in the evaluation report. Instruments should be chosen that have job-related content and appropriate norm groups so that both criterion-referenced and norm-referenced techniques can be incorporated into the interpretive process (Thomas, 1991).

An additional regulation governing the administration of tests reads as follows:

> It is unlawful for a covered entity to fail to select and administer tests concerning employment in the most effective manner to ensure that, when a test is administered to a job applicant or employee who has a disability that impairs sensory, manual or speaking skills, the test results accurately reflect the skills, aptitude, or whatever other factor of the applicant or employee that the test purports to measure, rather than reflecting the impaired sensory, manual, or speaking skills of such employee or applicant (except where such skills are the factors that the test purports to measure). (ADA, 1991, p. 35737)

This complex regulation emphasizes a point that should be of utmost concern to anyone using standardized instruments with rehabilitation clients. In short, it stresses the need carefully to choose and use tests and work samples that evaluate people's abilities rather than their disabilities. We must ensure that instruments are used and modified so that the outcomes are not influenced significantly by a disability. It is important to remember that as tests are modified, their standardization is compromised — any reliance on norms should be supplemented with other information resources (e.g., criterion-referenced interpretations, file review, interviews, use of other tests and work samples, situational assessment, occupational information).

CONTENT OF AN ADA-BASED VOCATIONAL EVALUATION REPORT

In cases where evaluation and assessment reports are required, the writer may want to ensure that information pertinent under the ADA is systematically presented. Narrative reports can be subheaded to reflect ADA content (e.g., Functional Strengths, Functional Limitations, Accommodations, Environmental Issues, Planning and Placement Contingencies, Recommendations). At a minimum, content within the various subheadings should cover the following points:

- A review of the functional strengths and limitations as they relate to various transitional/environmental settings and situations (e.g., transportation, home, community, work, activities of daily living, consumer skills)

- A discussion of how tests, work samples, and other assessment techniques were modified and their impact on performance

- An assessment of the client's ability to relate functional strengths and limitations to job tasks and to discuss appropriate accommodations for specific tasks with an employer

- A review of reasonable accommodation options and rehabilitation services that could be offered to overcome identified limitations related to placement recommendations

Before writing a report, reviewing the above points through a meeting with the client, referral source, and significant others helps refine recommendations, ensure consensus, and provide continuity in service delivery (Thomas, 1986).

CONCLUSION

The key to a successful ADA-based vocational evaluation or assessment is the accurate identification of functional strengths and limitations and the determination of reasonable accommodations that can minimize or eliminate the identified limitations. At times, the evaluation and assessment process has been criticized for doing little more than identifying limitations used to screen people out of services. The ADA still requires a focus on targeting limitations, but with the specific purpose of overcoming (accommodating) barriers to employment — the primary goal of the evaluation process.

Evaluators are not restricted by ADA guidelines when reviewing files, administering information questionnaires, or conducting interviews with clients, so that detailed information can be collected and used to formulate plans and recommendations that help clients function more effectively. However, the administration of standardized instruments should abide by the specific testing regulations of the ADA to maintain validity and eliminate adverse impact.

On the other hand, the creative and flexible use of work samples and situational assessment activities will permit the exploration of better ways to accommodate and match rehabilitation clients to various living and working environments. By their very nature, accommodations confound issues of standardization, and in these situations the psychometric properties of tests must give way to the diverse and unique needs of the person being evaluated. A balanced application of norm-referenced and criterion-referenced assessment strategies will result in a more holistic evaluation that truly reflects an individual's current functioning and future potential. Not only will the requirements of the ADA be met, but the opportunities for full integration of persons with disabilities into society will be realized.

REFERENCES

Adams, J. E. (1991). Judicial and regulatory interpretation of the employment rights of persons with disabilities. *Journal of Applied Rehabilitation Counseling, 22*, 28-46.

American Psychiatric Association. (1994). *Diagnostic and statistical manual of mental disorders* (4th ed.). Washington, DC: Author.

Americans with Disabilities Act–Part 1630. (Friday, July 26, 1991). Regulations to implement the equal employment provisions. *Federal Register*, Vol. 56, No. 144, pp. 35726-35753.

Anastasi, A. (1988). *Psychological testing* (6th ed.). New York: Macmillan.

Botterbusch, K. F. (1986). *A comparison of computerized job matching systems* (Rev. ed.). Menomonie, WI: University of Wisconsin-Stout, Materials Development Center.

Crewe, N. M., & Athelstan, G. T. (1984). *University of Minnesota: Functional assessment inventory manual.* Menomonie, WI: University of Wisconsin-Stout, Materials Development Center.

Drummond, R. J. (1988). *Appraisal procedures for counselors and helping professionals.* Columbus, OH: Merrill.

Farley, R. C., Little, N. D., Bolton, B., & Chunn, J. (N.D.). *Employment assessment & planning in rehabilitation & educational settings.* Hot Springs, AR: Arkansas Research & Training Center in Vocational Rehabilitation.

Field, J. E., & Field, T. F. (1992). *Revised classification of jobs.* Athens, GA: Elliot & Fitzpatrick.

Halpern, A. S., & Fuhrer, M. J. (1984). *Functional assessment in rehabilitation.* Baltimore: Paul H. Brookes.

Havranek, J., Grimes, J. W., Field, T., & Sink, J. (1994). *Vocational assessment: Evaluating employment potential.* Athens, GA: Elliot & Fitzpatrick.

Matarazzo, J. D. (1972). *Wechsler's measurement and appraisal of adult intelligence* (5th ed.). Baltimore: Williams & Wilkins.

Moon, S., Goodall, P., Barcus, M., & Brooke, V. (1986). *The supported work model of competitive employment for citizens with severe handicaps: A guide for job trainers* (Rev. ed.). Richmond, VA: Virginia Commonwealth University, Rehabilitation Research and Training Center.

Peterson, J. J. (1991). The impact of the ADA on the field of vocational evaluation. In R. R. Fry (Ed.), *Fifth national forum on issues in vocational assessment: The issues papers.* Menomonie, WI: University of Wisconsin-Stout, Materials Development Center.

Smith, A. (1988). *Symbol digit modalities test manual* (Rev. ed.). Los Angeles: Western Psychological Services.

Tenth Institute on Rehabilitation Issues. (1983). Dunbar, WV: Functional assessment. West Virginia Research and Training Center.

Thomas, S. W. (1986). *Writing on assessment and evaluation.* Menomonie, WI: University of Wisconsin-Stout, Materials Development Center.

Thomas, S. W. (1991). *Vocational evaluation and traumatic brain injury: A procedural manual.* Menomonie, WI: University of Wisconsin-Stout, Materials Development Center.

U. S. Department of Labor. (1991). *Dictionary of occupational titles* (4th ed., rev.). Indianapolis: Jist Works.

Vocational Rehabilitation Center of Allegheny County. (1983). *Specific learning disabilities: A resource manual.* Pittsburgh: Author.

Wechsler, D. (1970). *The measurement and appraisal of adult intelligence* (4th ed.). Baltimore: Williams & Wilkins.

Appendix 3A
RESOURCES ON THE ADA

Catalogues are available from the following organizations that contain publications on functional assessment instruments, reviews of standardized tests and work sample systems, occupational resource materials and software, and vocational evaluation and assessment procedures.

Arkansas Research and Training Center
in Vocational Rehabilitation
Publications Department
P. O. Box 1358
Hot Springs, AR 71902
(501) 624-4411, Ext. 316

Elliot & Fitzpatrick
P. O. Box 1945
Athens, GA 30603
(404) 548-8161

JIST Works, Inc.
720 North Park Avenue
Indianapolis, IN 46202-3431
(800) 648-5478

The Rehabilitation Resource
Stout Vocational Rehabilitation Institute
University of Wisconsin-Stout
Menomonie, WI 54751
(715) 232-1342

Research and Training Center
Stout Vocational Rehabilitation Institute
University of Wisconsin-Stout
Menomonie, WI 54751
(715) 232-1380

Virginia Commonwealth University
Rehabilitation Research and Training Center
VCU Box 2011
Richmond, VA 23284-0001
Attn: Resource Dissemination
(804) 257-1851

West Virginia Research and Training Center
One Dunbar Plaza, Suite E
Dunbar, WV 25064-3209
(304) 766-7138

4

Personal Assistance: A Key to Employability

Margaret A. Nosek, PhD, and Catherine Clubb Foley, PhD

Dr. Nosek is Associate Professor in the Department of Physical Medicine and Director of the Center for Research on Women with Disabilities; and Dr. Foley is Assistant Professor in the Department of Physical Medicine and Senior Researcher with the Center for Research on Women with Disabilities, Baylor College of Medicine, Houston, TX.

KEY POINTS

- *Personal assistance* is defined as assistance from another person in performing the activities of daily living to compensate for a functional limitation.

- Many Americans with disabilities have limited employment opportunities because they lack reliable, affordable personal assistance; in the United States, 7.7 million persons with disabilities require some assistance with day-to-day needs.

- The three levels of personal assistance are: minimal, moderate, and extensive.

- Seven categories of personal assistance options are available: family, spouse and family, family and hired assistant, full-time assistant, barter and multiple assistants, shared provider, and institution. In a study of these options, full-time personal assistant was rated the highest.

- Persons with disabilities must face difficult decisions about personal assistance and employment. These involve pride, finances, work site, level of need, and reasonable accommodations.

- Rehabilitation counselors can be of invaluable assistance by helping clients deal with fears, acquire information, plan arrangements, and understand the range of personal assistance options.

INTRODUCTION

A significant number of Americans with disabilities have limited employment opportunities because of a lack of reliable, affordable personal assistance. Rehabilitation counselors often see clients who receive state agency support for paid personal assistance services while they are in school; however, once they graduate, these clients are unable to secure employment salaries at levels that cover the expense of personal assistance services. In other situations, clients rely on family members for personal assistance during schooling due to a lack of funds; however, because of the continued lack of funds and an inexperience with management of nonfamily assistants, difficulties arise when persons with disabilities want to move away from home.

This chapter answers the following questions:

- What is personal assistance?

- How is it used by persons with disabilities?

- How effective are the various options for obtaining personal assistance?

- How does the availability of personal assistance affect employability?

Recommendations for rehabilitation counselors on how to assist their clients to meet personal assistance needs more effectively are provided.

WHAT IS PERSONAL ASSISTANCE?

Personal assistance is defined as assistance from another person in performing the activities of daily living to compensate for a functional limitation. For persons with severe disabilities, it means assistance (under maximum feasible control) with tasks aimed at maintaining well-being, personal appearance, comfort, safety, and interactions within the community and society as a whole. Personal assistance tasks are ones that persons would normally do for themselves if they did not have a disability (Litvak, Zukas, & Heumann, 1987).

The three levels of personal assistance are *minimal, moderate,* and *extensive.* The first level is for persons who could perform functions autonomously but choose to use assistance to conserve energy or time or to minimize discomfort or damage to weakened muscles. The second level is for persons who could perform functions autonomously in emergency situations but require assistance to manage with a reasonable degree of efficiency. The third level is for persons who could not perform survival functions alone under any circumstances.

In the United States, the estimated number of persons with disabilities who require some assistance with day-to-day needs is approximately 7.7 million (3.3% of the total population; Bureau of Economic Research and the World Institute on Disability, N.D.). Such persons within the working age range of 18–64 years number 3.16 million. Of persons who require personal assistance, 81% live with a relative or spouse, with 79% receiving unpaid help only.

WHAT OPTIONS FOR PERSONAL ASSISTANCE ARE AVAILABLE?

Seven broad categories of options are available for receiving personal assistance:

- *Family:* The most commonly used option is for the person to live with his or her family. In this situation, one (usually the mother) or both parents serve as the primary assistant(s), with supplemental assistance provided by other family members or neighbors and friends.

- *Spouse/Family:* The primary assistant is the spouse, with supplemental assistance provided by family members or friends.

- *Family/Hired Assistant:* In this situation, a combination of family members and persons are hired on a fee-for-service basis, with either being the primary assistant(s).

- *Full-Time Assistant:* One person provides all the needed personal assistance services for a majority of the week on a fee-for-service basis. Supplemental arrangements, for example on weekends, may be made.

- *Barter/Multiple Assistants:* In this situation, there may be some exchange of goods and services (such as room and board) for personal assistance. Neighbors, students, and persons from foreign countries without work permits comprise the traditional providers of this arrangement.

- *Shared Provider:* Two or more persons live together or in proximity and share the same assistant(s) for the needed combination of services. Service may be administered by the assistants or an agency.

- *Institution:* In this medical model category, an administrator oversees financial matters and provides services in a residential facility of six or more persons with disabilities.

HOW DO THESE OPTIONS RATE?

In 1988, 19 leaders in the independent living movement who used personal assistance services were asked to rate these options in terms of cost, risk incurred, quality of service, dignity afforded, and control (Table 4.1) (Nosek, 1992). A low score represented undesirable qualities, and a high score represented desirable qualities.

Table 4.1
RATING VARIOUS ARRANGEMENTS FOR RECEIVING PERSONAL ASSISTANCE

	Cost	Risk	Quality	Dignity	Control	*Total*	*Rank*
Full-time	2.8	4.1	4.4	4.5	4.6	20.4	1
Family and hired	3.5	3.6	3.8	3.8	3.4	18.1	2
Shared provider	3.5	3.2	3.2	3.7	3.0	16.6	3
Barter/multiple part-time	3.6	2.5	3.1	3.8	3.5	16.5	3
Spouse/family	3.6	3.3	3.4	2.9	2.9	16.1	3
Parents/family	3.4	3.2	3.5	2.9	2.5	15.5	4
Institution	1.7	2.4	1.9	1.3	1.3	8.6	5

n=19
Mean responses: 5 (very good) to 1 (very poor)

Averaged across all qualities, the option of a full-time personal assistant was rated the highest. Assistance from a combination of family members and hired persons was rated second overall but scored higher than full-time assistance on cost. Generally, three categories tied for third: shared provider, barter/multiple part-time assistants, and spouse/family. Some notable differences were evident: barter/multiple part-time scored lower on risk but higher than the others on control; the spouse/family option scored considerably lower on dignity and only scored slightly better than the other two on quality. Lower ratings on control caused the parents/

family option to be rated lower overall than these other three options. An institution was, by far, the least desirable choice.

A study of patients with spinal cord injury at the Baylor College of Medicine Research and Training Center on Spinal Cord Injury and Independent Living and Research Utilization revealed information about personal assistance usage patterns as reflected by living arrangement (with family, nonfamily, and alone) and assistance provider (family, nonfamily, and combination). Among the 286 patients with spinal cord injuries who used personal assistance and lived in the community, the largest segment—47%—lived with their families, who provided personal assistance (Table 4.2).

Table 4.2
ARRANGEMENTS FOR RECEIVING PERSONAL ASSISTANCE SERVICES AMONG PERSONS WITH SPINAL CORD INJURY (IN PERCENTAGES)

Living Arrangement	Family	Who Assists Nonfamily	Combination	*Total*
With family members	47	13	17	77
With nonfamily members	2	7	1	10
Alone	1	11	1	13
Total	50	31	19	100

n=286

Of the patients who worked full- or part-time (12%), nearly 60% employed persons outside the family did not live with them. The fact that these figures evidenced a higher percentage of nonfamily assistants than indicated by the Rutgers data suggests that patients with spinal cord injury are not completely representative of the disabled population. Experience dictates, however, that the trends identified are indicative of the disabled population as a whole.

The Issue of Funding:

Hiring nonfamily persons for personal assistance raises the

issue of available funds. For some persons, acquiring the funds to pay for personal assistance services is indeed difficult. According to the Rutgers profile, the population most in need of these services is the least able to pay for them through personal funds or private third-party payers. Most of these people do not have sufficient family resources, and public funding is the last resort. Furthermore, those with the most need are more likely to be unemployed; as a result of barriers in society that have led to unemployment, they generally have no insurance coverage and a lower overall family income.

Primary public sources of funding for personal assistance for working-aged persons include: Medicaid, Title XX, and Veterans benefits (Litvak et al., 1987). A much smaller, but growing, amount of money is available from special state programs and state/federal rehabilitation agencies (Nosek, 1989a, 1989b). Most of these funding resources have strict eligibility requirements. Until 1982, persons receiving supplemental Social Security income and Medicaid benefits lost funding for personal assistance services if they earned even minimal salaries. With the adoption into law of Section 1619 of the Social Security Act of 1982, such persons now can work and retain Medicaid personal assistance benefits.

WHAT EFFECT DOES PERSONAL ASSISTANCE HAVE ON EMPLOYABILITY?

Personal assistance is a linchpin service in meeting the survival and productivity needs of people with extensive functional limitations. For persons with less extensive needs, the relationship is less direct, but remains strong, nonetheless.

Employability is influenced by many factors, with support services representing only one. Other factors include skill level, intelligence, personality, social skills and behaviors, transportation availability, community accessibility, job market, and employer attitude. Although personal assistance enhances employability because it improves a person's ability to function in society, many characteristics of the existing service systems, as well as the general attitudes about receiving personal assistance, unfortunately confound the enhancement process.

Persons with disabilities must face various difficult decisions regarding personal assistance and employment. These involve pride, finances, work site, level of need, and reasonable accommodations.

Pride:

Similar to their nondisabled peers, many people with disabilities desire to become productive members of the workforce. Sometimes, employment changes the relationships between a person with a disability and his or her family, which leads to conflict of such dimensions that employment is terminated or the relationships are severely strained.

Finances:

When persons with disabilities have access to more money, they may desire to move out on their own as do their nondisabled peers. However, the prospect of losing public benefits may be a disincentive to employment. The realities of the job market may require relocation, a difficult prospect for a person who relies on family members and neighbors for a no-cost support system.

Work Site:

Transportation to the work site as well as the physical facilities at the site influence employability. Informal transportation arrangements may be acceptable for a volunteer position; however, with salaried employment, reliance on more costly, formal transportation may be required. Management of long distances at the work site may diminish the energy of some persons with disabilities.

Level of Need:

Certain levels of productivity may require more assistance than others, and the energy levels of persons with disabilities must be considered, both on and off the job. On the job, they may require assistance in manipulating files, books, or equipment. Because of depleted energy reserves during the workday, assistance at home for eating and bathing may be required.

Reasonable Accommodations:

Persons with disabilities requiring personal assistance have the right (under Title I of the Americans with Disabilities Act [ADA]) to ask their employers or potential employers to provide the services to meet these needs. Assistance with minor needs, such as opening doors or picking up an occasionally dropped object, should be treated as a common courtesy. However, if the need is more extensive, such as arranging work materials or manipulating equipment, it is better to have one person designated as an assistant, with this duty written into the job description. Assistance with personal tasks, such as preparing and eating lunch or using the restroom, should be treated formally and assigned as a job duty to someone who is on a lower rung in the organizational hierarchy than the person with the disability. It is the responsibility of the person with the disability to initiate a dialogue with the employer about the need for personal assistance on the job and the best way to meet that need.

ENHANCING EMPLOYABILITY RECOMMENDATIONS FOR REHABILITATION COUNSELORS

Rehabilitation counselors can enhance the employability of their clients by incorporating goals that are related to improving personal assistance arrangements in their individualized, written rehabilitation plans. Some guidelines for assessing a client's situation and effecting such improvements follow.

Assess the Adequacy of Current Arrangements:

Adequacy should be considered in terms of client control, quality, availability, and cost. Survival needs are only minimum needs; they may not be convenient or conducive to health or productivity and may not afford the client the desired level of control. The degree of reliance on aging family members or on others who desire to pursue their own goals should be explored. Frequently occurring health problems may signal an inadequate arrangement. For example, a client may need to make more trips to the bathroom than he or she can make alone, but may be unaware of ways to arrange and pay for assistance at certain times during the day; or a client may develop pressure ulcers if no assistance is available for turning him or her at night.

The Personal Assistance Satisfaction Index (Nosek, Potter, & Quan, 1992) consists of 16 items specific to various aspects of personal assistance; the items are rated on a 5-point Likert scale, ranging from "not at all satisfied" to "very satisfied." Clients and counselors can use the instrument to identify weak areas in personal assistance arrangements. The areas of personal assistance covered include the perceived amount of control over assistance received, quality of assistance along a variety of dimensions, availability of assistance (hours of the day), location, type of task, cost of service, its reasonableness in terms of price of service, and availability of funds to purchase needed services.

Determine Whether a Change Is Necessary or Desirable:

Once employment has been secured, it may become evident that the current arrangements for personal assistance are not adequate. In such a situation, transition planning should be initiated. The first step is to specify what is required. Scheduling needs, prioritizing tasks, arranging for family and hired assistance, and planning for backup services must be considered. For example, with regard to bodily functions, it is important to know to what extent they can be regulated through monitoring fluid intake.

There are four basic categories of assistance needs: (a) bodily functions (bathing, toileting, dressing, eating); (b) household duties (cleaning, cooking, laundering); (c) mobility (driving, pushing a wheelchair); and (d) communication (interpreting speech, writing, reading). Each of these categories can be assigned a rating along a scale from essential for survival to essential for safety, comfort, and productivity to desirable but not essential. Of course, tasks that can be performed autonomously without undue fatigue, time expenditure, or safety risk save anxiety and money when it comes to personal assistance service. It is important to explore individual levels of independent functioning. More details on the process of identifying such needs are available on audiotape from The Institute for Rehabilitation and Research (Nosek, 1989a).

Identify Relevant Preferences and Abilities:

Once the client's needs have been identified, prioritized, and quantified, the next step is to help him or her determine specific preferences and take an honest look at how personality, habits, and self-direction might influence the success of personal assistance arrangements. Because conversations of this intensity require a close and confidential relationship, rushed or *pro forma* discussions should be avoided. When counselors reveal some of their own experiences, clients are encouraged to verbalize their own. This exercise can enhance clients' perceptions of independence and help them develop a support system for productivity based on their own circumstances. Sample questions counselors might ask include:

- Do you prefer your current arrangements, or would you like to make any changes?

- How emotionally dependent are you on your family?

- How well do you tolerate risk or uncertainty?

- How important to you is privacy?

- Can you learn to manage or direct others who help you?

The seven options for personal assistance outlined previously can be addressed with the client to encourage an honest discussion about fears, anticipated problems, and preferences.

Explore Methods for Meeting Needed Services:

Cost is the critical factor in determining the feasibility of options for personal assistance. Qualifications for public funds as well as the provisions of the Rehabilitation Act of 1973 (Title I [vocational rehabilitation services], Title VI [supported employment], and Title VII [independent living]) can be explored. Funding under Title I of the ADA from employers for assistance on the job should be considered, too. When a client's income exceeds the limits imposed by eligibility criteria for public sources of support, it becomes necessary to draw on private sources, such as salary or family financial support, or to find other economical methods to meet these needs.

Redesign Arrangements:

At this time, no national personal assistance service system exists. This makes the job of improving arrangements difficult for individuals with disabilities and helping professionals. In communities with an independent living center, assistance may be available through the center's independent living skills classes (for personal assistant management training), peer counseling (to learn how others meet personal assistance needs), or personal assistant referral. Some centers have a transitional living component for intense skills training and options exploration.

The psychological make-up of the client as well as available resources influence whether a sudden or gradual approach to changing arrangements is best. With a sudden approach, a backup system is especially important. When the gradual approach is taken and former assistance resources (such as family members) are too easily accessible, there is little incentive to endure the inevitable difficult times that come with any substantial life change. When new needs arise because of living or employment arrangements, there may be a change in help-seeking behaviors. For example, employees with disabilities may seek the natural support of other employees. Although this avenue might be appropriate for minor tasks that do not impose significant interruptions, it is not appropriate for recurring, intimate, or substantial tasks. Relationships and work performance may be affected, especially when help is sought from subordinates, who may feel pressured to assist.

All employers, except for those with fewer than fifteen employees, are required under the ADA to provide reasonable accommodations for the employment-related needs of their workers. Substantial needs — modifying job requirements, purchasing equipment, hiring a personal assistant, or including personal assistance in the job description of another employee — may be arranged formally with the employer. Rehabilitation counselors can explain to clients their rights to reasonable accommodations and help them develop assertiveness skills to request such appropriate accommodations.

Develop a Backup Support System:

No system is foolproof. Therefore, the best way to ensure maximum security is to establish a strong backup support network. For clients with extensive needs who prefer highly secure arrangements, a shared provider system might be considered. An agency or other entity would be responsible for selecting and scheduling assistants. With this arrangement, there is a give and take between control and security. For clients who can tolerate more risk, a system of agreements between friends, neighbors, family members, and even employers is adequate for emergency situations. However, if the backup network is used too often, it may be necessary to change assistants or arrangements. A backup network is crucial to maintain the level of social functioning demanded by employment.

CONCLUSION

Personal assistance is a key factor in compensating for the difference between an individual's level of physical functioning and the functional demands of employment. Whether an employee appears on time for work entirely autonomously or with assistance from an elaborate system makes no difference to an employer. The demands of dealing with the emotional and financial aspects of personal assistance are considerable and require substantial attention during the rehabilitation process. Rehabilitation counselors can be of invaluable assistance to clients by helping them deal with fears, acquiring information, planning arrangements, and understanding the range of personal assistance options.

REFERENCES

Bureau of Economic Research and the World Institute on Disability. (N.D.). *Towards an understanding of the demand for personal assistance.* New Brunswick, NJ: Rutgers University.

Litvak, S., Zukas, H., & Heumann, J. E. (1987). *Attending to America: Personal assistance for independent living: A survey of attendant services programs in the United States for people of all ages with disabilities.* Berkeley, CA: World Institute on Disability.

Nosek, M. (Speaker). (1989a). *Busting loose to independence through personal attendant services* [Cassette Recording]. Houston, TX: The Institute for Rehabilitation and Research.

Nosek, M. (1989b). *Expanding attendant care options for disabled Texans: A source book.* Houston, TX: Independent Living and Research Utilization.

Nosek, M. (1992). The personal assistance dilemma for people with disabilities living in rural areas. *Rural Special Education Quarterly, 11,* 36-40.

Nosek, M., Potter, C., & Quan, H. (1992). *The personal assistance satisfaction index.* Houston, TX: Independent Living and Research Utilization.

5

Placement Practices and Labor Markets for Clients with Disabilities

David Vandergoot, PhD, CRC

Dr. Vandergoot is the President of the Center for Essential Management Services, Oceanside, NY; and Faculty Member, Hunter College, New York, NY.

KEY POINTS

- Job placement of persons with disabilities should be a serious concern of all vocational rehabilitation professionals.

- Complementing placement services with comprehensive marketing strategies enhances the resources directed at finding employment opportunities for persons with disabilities.

- Incentives that rehabilitation programs can offer employers include: low cost access to job candidates, applicants who are prescreened, and follow-up support for long-term success. The main reason for serving employers is to ensure that they hire the right person for any given job.

- Understanding how labor markets work equips vocational rehabilitation counselors with a framework for designing services and program management strategies sensitive to the needs of persons with disabilities *and* employers.

- Placement models vary in perspective; all have useful components. Some models, such as *competitive* and *supported employment*, affect the supply side of the labor market, whereas others, such as *projects with industry*, focus on affecting the demand side.

- General recommendations are given for implementing placement services and organizing and administering placement programs.

THE EMPLOYMENT NEEDS OF CLIENTS WITH DISABILITIES

In 1988, census data reported that approximately 13.5 million persons between the ages of 16 and 64 had a work disability (Bennefield & McNeil, 1989), which amounts to about 8.6% of the U.S. population. Of these, 7.5 million (4.8%) had severe disabilities. Only 32% of those reporting a disability, however, were working; and a mere 10.2% of persons with severe disabilities were represented in the workforce. Only 3 of every 10 men with disabilities and 2 of 10 women with disabilities of working age were employed full-time (U.S. Bureau of the Census, 1986). This lack of participation in the workforce by those with disabilities as compared with those in the general population is further documented by the following statistics from the 1980s (Bennefield & McNeil, 1989):

- 36% of men with disabilities were in the workforce compared with 89% of men in general

- 23% of men with disabilities worked full-time compared with 75% of men in general

- The unemployment rate was 14.2% for men with disabilities, whereas it was 6.2% for men in general

- 27.5% of women with disabilities were in the workforce compared with 70% of women without disabilities

- Only 13% of women with disabilities worked full-time, whereas 47.1% of women without disabilities did so

- The unemployment rate for women with disabilities was 14.2%, whereas it was 5.2% for women in general

- Income for persons with disabilities lagged behind that of others and increased at a slower rate

- Although persons with disabilities comprised 8.6% of the population, they comprised 21.9% of persons at or below the poverty level

- 52% of employed men with disabilities were covered by employer-sponsored health plans, whereas 66% of men in general were covered; for women, the rates were 40% and 53%, respectively

The Louis Harris (1986) poll commissioned by the National Council on Disability confirmed in more graphic detail the problems persons with disabilities face as a result of their lack of participation in the economic and social mainstream. This national survey found that only 25% of working-age persons with disabilities work full-time, with another 10% employed part-time. Two thirds of those not working said they would accept employment if it were offered. Although disability itself was attributed by respondents as the major barrier to employment, 47% indicated that employers did not recognize their ability to work full-time. In addition, 40% indicated a lack of knowledge regarding how to find jobs; 38% felt they did not have the skills, education, and training to get a full-time job; 28% attributed unemployment to lack of accessible transportation; and 23% indicated that they would need special devices or accommodations to work.

People with disabilities do not reach the 50% rate of participation in the workforce at any age, and, as they become older, their participation rates decline ever more steeply (U.S. Bureau of the Census, 1986). Annually, over 500,000 Americans experience a disability that keeps them out of work for at least 5 months (Hester & Decelles, 1985). Only about 48% of workers who leave their jobs and enter disability support systems return to work; 36% "retire" due to disability, and 16% die (National Institute on Disability and Rehabilitation Research, 1989).

The incidence and prevalence of disability suggested in these statistics will continue to rise as medical breakthroughs help people live longer. The National Institute on Aging projects a 53% increase in the number of people in disability support systems and rehabilitation programs in the next three decades (Rickard, 1985). Given that this statistical outlook has existed for many years without substantial improvement, placement must become a serious concern of all vocational rehabilitation professionals.

LABOR MARKETS AS A CONCEPTUAL FRAMEWORK

It is helpful to recognize that placement occurs when a person is offered, and then accepts, a job; an employer has to make a decision to select an applicant, and an applicant has to decide to accept the job offer. This type of search is conducted in labor markets. To understand how placement occurs and to plan services that take advantage of how labor markets work, it is necessary to understand labor markets as a concept.

In essence, labor markets are simply mechanisms to put the right persons in the right jobs. Just as supermarkets exist to assist people in obtaining desired foods quickly and easily, labor markets exist to help select the appropriate people for the appropriate jobs. Note that two decisions must be made: (a) to whom to offer a job and (b) whether to accept a job offer. Thus, two decision makers are necessary: (a) employers who select applicants and (b) applicants who select employers. Employers create the demand for workers and applicants comprise the supply of workers available to fulfill the demand. Labor markets help employers and applicants manage their respective decisions.

If supermarkets provide the opportunity for persons to select food in exchange for money, what is exchanged in labor markets? One way of looking at this is to view *decisions* as the products that employers and applicants desire to obtain from the labor market. Information is exchanged to make decisions.

The quality of decisions improves with the investment in information. However, obtaining information carries a cost, and applicants and employers want to make the best decisions without bearing excessive costs. Because employers use many sources to create an applicant pool, they incur many costs when recruiting and hiring workers. Even though rehabilitation agencies, as one source in this pool, do not charge employers for placing an applicant, agencies still must show that they can reduce employer costs in other ways.

PLACEMENT MODELS

Current placement models overlap considerably; the only major difference is one of perspective. One viewpoint focuses on the role of counselors. *Selective placement* denotes an approach in which counselors actively persuade employers to provide opportunities to persons with disabilities. Counselors bear most of the responsibility for organizing all needed services. The disabled person (the consumer) is usually not active in the process leading up to employment, except as the recipient of services. A contrasting view is described as *client-centered placement*. Under this model, the counselor is nondirective and acts as a facilitator or teacher who enables the consumer to select and pursue services and employment as independently as possible; in client-centered placement, most of the outreach to employers is done by clients themselves.

A second perspective for describing placement models is based on a service delivery approach. *Competitive placement* refers to a train–place–follow-up process that leads to employment. This approach reflects traditional vocational rehabilitation in which most services are provided before employment, usually in special, segregated settings designed for persons with disabilities. In contrast, *supported placement* uses a place–train–follow-up approach to service delivery. This model provides most services in work establishments after employment is obtained. These settings are integrated; they combine persons with disabilities and workers without disabilities. A rehabilitation service provider brings services to consumers in the community rather than requiring them to travel to special facilities.

Competitive and *supported placement* affect the supply side of labor markets in that they are designed to enable persons with disabilities to compete with others for jobs. Gilbride and Stensrud (1992) suggest that a third perspective is necessary — one that has an impact on the *demand* side of labor markets. Such a model would actually create jobs for persons with disabilities through active interventions initiated with businesses. The focus of change would be the work environment as opposed to persons with disabilities. The *projects with industry* (PWI) model incorporates several aspects of this approach. PWIs are employer-rehabilitation partnership programs that seek mutual ways to fulfill organizational needs by providing employment for persons with disabilities. The Americans with Disabilities Act (ADA) provides additional opportunities for promoting these demand-side models (Gilbride & Stensrud, 1992). Rehabilitation professionals can provide employers with valuable services for which businesses are willing to pay because they are required by the ADA.

All of these models have useful ingredients and have made an impact on labor markets on behalf of persons with disabilities. It is now possible to envision a more complete model that carefully balances the attention of rehabilitation professionals across the supply *and* demand sides of labor markets.

PLACEMENT SERVICES FOR EMPLOYERS

In any situation, the agency must remember that it is not the sole provider of services for an employer. Indeed, competition pervades all layers of labor markets. Being able to help employers wisely manage costs provides the best opportunity for rehabilitation professionals to facilitate the employment of persons with disabilities. The challenge facing rehabilitation professionals is to optimize outcomes for disabled persons and employers at the same time. With success, their role will become increasingly valuable to employers, clients with disablities, and society as a whole.

Employers want to obtain productive workers through an efficient and effective hiring process. Incentives that rehabilitation programs can offer employers include:

- Low-cost access to job candidates

- Applicants who are prescreened

- Follow-up support for long-term success

Research confirms that these are important expectations that employers hold for rehabilitation programs (Vandergoot, Staniszewski, & Gany, 1993; Young, Rosati, & Vandergoot, 1986). This same research, however, indicates that employers' expectations are not met completely. In these studies, employers who were experienced users of rehabilitation services responded that more could have been done by rehabilitation programs to serve them. All efforts to serve employers should be explained in terms of how the above expectations can be met by the services provided. It must not be forgotten that the chief reason for serving employers is to ensure that they hire the right person for any given job.

Figure 5.1 illustrates that many employers did not receive desired services and that almost one fourth of those who had received placement support were not entirely satisfied. These employers were probably the best customers of rehabilitation services because many of them had hired more than one person with a disability through rehabilitation programs. Employers are not being served well enough in two important areas: the hiring process and the provision of follow-up support.

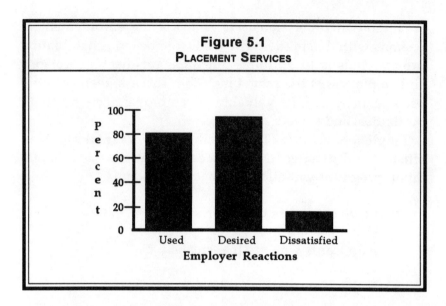

Figure 5.1
PLACEMENT SERVICES

How do we interpret these results for use in daily practice? First, all services provided to employers should be justified in one of two ways. Service should be directed either toward helping the employer hire the right person or, once the person is hired, providing the appropriate follow-up. The labor market model suggests that the place–train or place–train-maintain supported employment models of service delivery make the most sense.

Second, the rehabilitation field, as a whole, is not providing follow-up support to the degree needed and desired by employers. With the growth of supported employment, this expectation might be met to a greater degree than at any time before. Supported employment has also defined the types of support that can be included in follow-up: co-worker instruction, crisis intervention, job modification, site accommodations, and identification and use of natural work site supports (e.g., co-worker mentors and transportation assistance). Any service that overcomes a job-related problem—even family counseling dealing with domestic problems that interfere with job success—should be offered. Visionary delivery approaches developed through supported employment should be extended to all types of placements. Employers do not distinguish between competitive and supported jobs. The important thing to them is that all of their jobs are performed at the most profitable competitive rates possible.

PLACEMENT SERVICES FOR CLIENTS WITH DISABILITIES

Most people who come to vocational rehabilitation programs do so because they want to work (Roessler & Schriner, 1991). Of course, some people are unmotivated to work and, regardless of what services are provided, they are not likely to be placed. Other persons will not be employed because they do not have the appropriate labor market skills.

Table 5.1 portrays the variety of behaviors that employers feel contribute to the success of a worker (Vandergoot et al., 1993). These behaviors and skills include more than just the ability to complete job tasks in a productive fashion. Table 5.1 also compares workers with disabilities in supported and competitive placement with a hypothetical average worker. (The workers in competitive placement had high potential and were assumed not to need supported employment.) The average worker, by definition, is rated a "2" on a 3-point scale. For example, on productivity and work skills, supported workers are rated somewhat below competitive workers with disabilities who are rated on a par with the average worker in these areas. Despite lower ratings, supported workers are rated overall as only slightly lower than the average worker, whereas competitively placed workers with disabilities are rated higher.

Employers evidently value a variety of work skills and behaviors other than performance on job tasks. Better-than-average performance in other areas can compensate for less-than-average work skills. Employers rated supported workers highly in attendance, punctuality, and dependability. This suggests that a good performance in these areas can compensate for diminished productivity. A balance among these behaviors is required of a person to be a highly marketable candidate for placement.

Table 5.1
EMPLOYERS' COMPARISON OF SUPPORTED WORKERS WITH OTHER WORKERS

Performance Category	Average Worker	Supported Worker	Competitive Worker
Social integration with co-workers during breaks, lunch	2.0	1.8	2.0
Social integration with co-workers during regular work hours	2.0	1.8	2.0
General appearance	2.0	2.0	2.1
Compatibility with supervisors	2.0	1.9	2.1
Compliance with instructions	2.0	1.8	2.1
Punctuality in arrival to and departure from work	2.0	2.3	2.4
Productivity	2.0	1.6	2.0
Safety/accident prevention	2.0	2.0	2.2
Dependability	2.0	2.2	2.4
Attendance	2.0	2.4	2.5
Work skills	2.0	1.6	2.0
Work habits	2.0	1.8	2.1
Work attitudes	2.0	1.8	2.1
Overall work performance	2.0	1.8	2.3

Job-Seeking Skills:

Aside from work performance skills, employers indicated that they value applicants who can demonstrate good job-seeking skills (Young et al., 1986). Employers seem to use ability in this area to indicate work potential if that cannot be measured directly. Thus, given this input from employers, rehabilitation professionals need to provide services to equip consumers with a variety of on-the-job skills and job-seeking ability. These are relatively independent and require different behaviors and knowledge.

Work Readiness:

As consumers become more skillful, they increase their work readiness. Much effort has been devoted to defining the concept of work readiness and how to quantify it. However, readiness is a relative concept that can only be defined by the unique interaction between a potential employee and employers in the labor market. Theoretically, a person is work ready when he or she can do one particular job. However, the odds of finding that job are slim. The more jobs a person is "ready" for, the more likely he or she will become employed, although there is no optimal profile of work readiness that a consumer should have before placement is attempted. Improving readiness has diminishing returns.

Skill Building:

Skill building should begin with evaluation and assessment to determine the disabled client's current functioning and knowledge. How a person learns best also should be determined so that service delivery can be tailored to this person's unique needs. Knowing how to do this will also be useful when working with an employer to develop any necessary accommodations required by the ADA.

THE EVALUATION PROCESS

If a person has a work history, the evaluation process should begin with an analysis of transferability of skills (Kaiser, 1983). This can be a shortcut to identifying previously developed skills that can be applied to other occupations. Care must be taken to adjust the level of these skills on the basis of current functioning abilities, which may have been modified due to the onset or profession of disability since the earlier work was performed.

Transferability analysis can be greatly facilitated by computerized systems. The results can be as useful as those from a complete vocational evaluation and are more cost and time efficient (Tooman, 1982). Moreover, transferability analysis can point to areas requiring more thorough assessment methods. It also reduces the time and cost of an evaluation by eliminating assessment of functional areas that are already documented by the transferability analysis. Another useful feature of transferability analysis is its potential to present a variety of future labor market possibilities to consumers based on different training or education strategies. These "what if" scenarios can be helpful in selecting service options that have the best payoff for meeting short- and long-range needs of consumers.

For persons without a work history, more traditional evaluation approaches must be applied to provide an opportunity to explore their potential in the labor market. A foremost principle of any evaluation is that findings should be used to identify the full range of available labor market possibilities. Findings should not be applied to limit options. Whereas the labor market is designed to narrow the range of jobs for which a person can compete, the rehabilitation process should expand options so that consumers can pursue as many jobs as possible, thus increasing their chances of finding an appropriate position.

THE JOB PLACEMENT PROCESS

Developing a Rehabilitation Plan:

Early on, rehabilitation counselors should help clients identify the needs they hope to meet through obtaining work. This will facilitate placement by indicating the features of jobs that will meet consumer needs, such as income, hours, and location. These are general parameters that can be met by many different types of jobs in many different industries. Of course, clients have other needs that should not be discounted, such as finding jobs that meet their interests, skills, and career ambitions. Fulfilling these needs, however, depends on information that is not likely to be available early in the rehabilitation process. As consumers become more knowledgeable about labor market opportunities, they can make better judgments regarding these other needs. The rehabilitation process should work to expand horizons, because the labor market will narrow options to the one job a consumer will eventually obtain.

Financial Needs of the Client:

Framing objectives in terms of income needs is recommended because financial needs are frequently compelling. Many clients risk losing disability income and medical benefits if they become employed. A critical decision involves determining whether or not work will pay off: will the income such workers earn offset the loss of disability and medical benefits as well as the costs associated with working (e.g., transportation, clothing, and food expenses)? Perhaps many consumers become unmotivated when they realize that work may not be worthwhile because the jobs available to them do not improve their finances. By determining their income and benefit needs and by estimating the income they could earn given their current capabilities (i.e., their current value in the labor market), a benchmark is established to determine if they can obtain suitable jobs or if additional training, education, and skill building will be needed. A strong incentive for motivation is to show the client how participation in rehabilitation activities can increase income potential. Although people desire to work for reasons other than just salary, receiving an income is an essential need that predominates over others. Needs associated with income generally must be met before needs such as personal interests and achieving social status are fulfilled.

Assessing and Teaching Job Skills:

After standards are set and the range of labor market skills is identified, it is possible to proceed in assessing and teaching job skills in preparation for placement. This typical phase of the rehabilitation program can be circumvented, however, for three reasons. First, most employers expect to provide orientation — and even training — to new employees if they have met basic entry requirements. They will do this regardless of the prior training employees have had. Rehabilitation training programs, although they provide valuable skills, often cannot give the person the specific skills unique to a particular employer; such skills must be learned on the job. Second, experience with supported employment documents the willingness of employers to allow rehabilitation training resources to be used on the job. On-the-job training (OJT) is an extremely powerful training technique. Third, more formal approaches to training are not as successful. Studies have documented that over half of all placements after training are not related to what was trained previously (Chun & Growick, 1983).

Completing a training program, however, does appear to be valuable to employers, even though what was learned may not necessarily matter. Completing a training program indicates that a person can learn successfully and is willing to persist until a job is complete. Therefore, training should be considered in those cases in which it can substantially increase the odds that someone may become employed. Training is also important if only certain kinds of jobs can provide for the income needs of a consumer.

For several reasons, on-the-job training is preferable. Training should take place in a rehabilitation setting only as a last resort. First, optimal performance usually does not depend on transfer of learning from the learning environment to the criterion environment in which the learned skills are to be performed. OJT is obviously superior in this regard because no transfer is required. If OJT is not possible, community-based training programs such as those found in adult or vocational education programs, community and 4-year colleges, and technical/business institutes should be considered. Also, these programs usually have greater resources to keep training standards in line with current labor market demands that are often difficult for disability-specific programs to achieve.

The Job Search:

Job-seeking skills instruction can begin at any point in the process, but it typically commences when training or other skill-building activities are coming to an end. Many commercial packages are available for facilitating these skills. Group instruction is possible, but individual needs must be considered. Some consumers will be able to learn on their own by using self-study guides; others will require intensive one-on-one tutoring.

Different labor markets require different search skills. Accordingly, job search skills instruction must be tailored for labor markets. Instructional packages typically do not account for such specification.

The job-seeking process should be initiated by the development of formal placement plans that document the full set of objectives to be achieved including income, location, and types of jobs desired. Companies to be contacted should be listed, including which contacts are to be made by the counselor or placement specialist. The extent of contacts, as well as the time frame in which they are to be made, should be indicated to ensure that accountability is incorporated into the process.

The job search should be intensive. The rehabilitation plan becomes a contract between the client and counselor by reinforcing the importance of job search activities, specifying responsibilities and due dates, and requiring signatures of both the job searcher and professional. The plan should specify activities for only several weeks and should include checkpoints for the client and counselor to review progress, share information, and make revisions in the plan based on new information. The search should be broad and the plan flexible to take full advantage of new labor market knowledge. It is not unusual for original vocational objectives to be modified as a result of job searching that reveals new labor market opportunities that had not been anticipated. If a job offer is obtained, the original objectives pertaining to income, location, and other needs can be used as a standard to see if the offer is adequate. How well one job offer matches the consumer's original objectives can help the individual decide whether or not to accept the job.

The job search can be difficult in terms of the time and effort required. It is also a potentially threatening process because a job seeker faces numerous personal evaluations that may often result in rejection; this can seriously diminish motivation to continue. Clarifying expectations based on typical labor market experiences is one way of dealing with this threat. Job searchers need to recognize that, on average, many contacts are needed to obtain one offer. Rejections are to be expected. But each rejection reveals new information to be used in further searching and also brings the person one step closer to an actual offer. Job searchers must realize that this is how labor markets work and that they are not to take rejection personally.

Follow-up Services:

Once a placement occurs, the counselor has the opportunity to serve the client and employer simultaneously by providing follow-up services. A contact schedule should be arranged in advance with both parties, particularly if the counselor had a prior relationship with the employer. If the consumer found the job on his or her own, the counselor must get the person's permission before following up with the employer. Scheduled contacts can usually be made by telephone, which saves everyone's time.

The counselor also must be available to handle emergencies or unforeseen circumstances for which the person or employer requests help. The ability to respond to requests from both parties separates the rehabilitation counselor from other employment resources available to employers. Being able to assist with follow-up over a reasonable period of time will do much to ensure repeat placements.

Developing a Plan for Career Development:

One final placement function is to work with the client to develop a plan for career development. As with the placement plan, this plan should specify career objectives and action steps for achieving them. Obviously, the rehabilitation counselor will have less responsibility in fulfilling this plan than the placement plan. The major responsibility rests with the client, and, to some extent, with the employer. However, any assistance given by the counselor (e.g., pointing out to the employer how additional accommodations can be made) is desirable.

RECOMMENDATIONS FOR PLACEMENT PRACTICE FROM THE RESEARCH LITERATURE

In an extensive review of the literature, Vandergoot (1987) described research findings from the previous two decades that have implications for placement practice. These findings suggest ways to implement services as well as how programs can be organized and administered. Briefly, these major findings are:

- Placement should be made an explicit priority for service staff. Top management should communicate this by setting performance requirements, establishing placement target goals, and rewarding staff based on their contributions to the placement effort.

- Formal evaluation strategies, such as paper-and-pencil testing, should be superseded by techniques that reflect principles of situational assessment and evaluate persons on real tasks, in real environments, and in real time.

- Vocational goals set by the client should be broad at the outset to avoid pigeonholing the client into one job type. The labor market is designed to narrow a person's search to one job. The rehabilitation process should not do that prematurely and deprive a consumer of the feedback obtained through interaction with the labor market.

- Place–train approaches are more congruent with how labor markets function. Employers expect to train new employees, and training is more successful when transfer of knowledge is minimized.

- Employers have indicated a need for assistance after a placement beyond what rehabilitation professionals can provide. Given the limited resources available to vocational rehabilitation systems, placement success is more likely if more energy is spent preparing a person to be successful *after* placement than investing in training before placement. This should apply to all clients rather than solely to those in supported employment.

- Job development should occur in the context of building employer partnerships. It should not be a one-shot enterprise to secure a job for a specific consumer, especially if the employer is unknown. Placing a consumer at an unfamiliar work site can result in a good match only by chance and does not reinforce the notion that rehabilitation professionals are labor market experts. Job development should focus on referring persons to an employer only if there is a good likelihood that they offer what the employer needs and that the employer offers what they need. These referrals are needed especially by persons who do not have the resources to participate in independent job search activities.

- Formal placement plans that detail responsibilities of both the client with a disability and the rehabilitation professional are useful for improving placement performance. These plans guide and organize the efforts of both parties and give an edge to participants in a rehabilitation program because the search processes used by others tend to be haphazard. When plans are revised on a regular basis, consumers have opportunities to apply what they learn from their searching and redirect their efforts to take advantage of new opportunities.

THE USE OF MARKETING TECHNIQUES

In the past, the rehabilitation field has explored how marketing can be used to develop more productive relationships with employers, mainly through job development and various media appeals. However, broader applications of marketing are possible and have the potential to benefit rehabilitation programs in many more ways. Appropriate use of marketing requires an organization to systematically identify its purposes based on the needs of its customers. A marketing-conscious organization is able to state its mission and goals clearly, develop services that effectively achieve these purposes, and communicate them to the varied audiences on which it depends.

Applying marketing strategies is particularly useful with employers. After all, marketing is a business tool. Business people understand the value of marketing, and the language of marketing can serve as a common denominator between employers and rehabilitation professionals. Describing rehabilitation programs to employers in marketing terms enables them to understand how rehabilitation programs can assist them with their labor market needs. The fact that both rehabilitation and business depend on labor markets for a significant portion of their success reinforces the idea that using marketing strategies within a labor market context is conceptually sound. With the passage of the ADA, employers have a second need for assistance: rehabilitation professionals can market themselves as teachers who can provide assistance in complying with ADA regulations (see Chapter 3).

Marketing to employers can be defined as an ongoing approach that enables vocational rehabilitation agencies to identify employer needs, refocus resources and management structures, and improve services to people with disabilities and employers who satisfy these needs. The goal of marketing to employers is to establish long-term partnerships that will lead to more and better job opportunities for persons with disabilities. Rehabilitation agencies that adopt a marketing philosophy understand that they must serve several customers, including those with disabilities and employers who will eventually hire many of these persons. Referral sources, vendors, and professionals such as physicians are examples of clients with whom the agency needs to develop mutually satisfying relationships. Therefore, a rehabilitation agency guided by a marketing philosophy will move from an organizational focus to a customer focus. It will frame its goals in terms of the needs of its major audiences. Moreover, using marketing approaches can redefine problems faced by agencies and suggest new ways of solving them.

Specifically, a marketing-conscious agency:

- Recognizes that it has value if it adequately meets the needs of its customers

- Holds itself responsible for its failures and does not blame its customers (i.e., "unmotivated clients" and "prejudiced" or "ignorant" employers)

- Conducts ongoing research to identify the needs of

important customers, and collects data to evaluate how well these needs are met

- Uses public relations strategies to communicate its mission and value to customers

- Requires that all staff understand how their functions contribute to marketing because all staff should perform in ways that meet the needs of employers and people with disabilities

- Develops a marketing strategy for each of its important customer groups

- Provides services that enable the agency to meet needs in a way that competing agencies cannot

COMPONENTS OF THE MARKETING PROCESS

The three components of marketing are: (a) environmental assessment, (b) strategic planning, and (c) implementation. Although described separately here, these components are interdependent. They comprise the marketing process and form the core of a philosophy and concern for customers that must permeate the entire agency.

Environmental Assessment:

Environmental assessment is a continuous process conducted to reveal significant or unexpected changes in the internal and external environments that might affect the agency. Environmental assessment includes identifying opportunities (or benefits) and threats (or risks) presented by environmental forces that influence the ability of an organization to attain its goals. The purpose of this assessment is to help an organization adjust to changing customer needs.

To build partnerships with employers that result in job opportunities for persons with disabilities, agency personnel need to be aware of how employers currently meet their labor market needs. They also should know employers' perceived risks and benefits for being partners with a vocational rehabilitation agency as compared with other sources of job applicants.

There are two ways that environmental assessments can be approached — through environmental "scans" and more formal marketing research. An environmental scan is an informal, ongoing process to identify and act proactively to events in the environment. As applied to developing a marketing strategy for employers, an environmental scan might focus on identifying and monitoring external factors that affect the agency's ability to supply sufficient, appropriate jobs for clients. Factors include local and national economic, political, and social forces. Information about competitors, technologic changes, and clients may also be relevant. Agency personnel might want to keep a close watch on referral sources, labor market trends, and the changing nature of the demographic composition of the local population.

Similar to scanning, marketing research gathers data on environmental forces. Environmental scanning, however, is used to raise questions, whereas marketing research is designed to provide answers. As a formal process, it follows a problem-solving structure using quantitative methods appropriate to the question at hand. It plays a critical role in understanding the behavior of outside influences and in planning customer-related activities; it ranges from conducting simple, one-time analyses of easily accessed documents to complex, long-term, or repetitive experiments. It can rely on low-cost techniques or involve considerable expense.

Strategic Planning:

Strategic planning has been heralded as the key to successful management. In fact, managers in the public and nonprofit sectors have been encouraged to adopt this management style. When executed properly, strategic planning creates a vision of the agency's mission that all managers and staff can personalize. Furthermore, staff can use this vision to guide their daily activities.

The key ingredients to successful strategic planning are participation, communication, and action. Representatives from all departments and units should work together to formulate this overall agency vision. Writing the plan, however, cannot be viewed as an end in itself. In fact, writing the plan is the easy part. Too often, having this document in place seems sufficient. The true value of the written plan will be realized when managers and other staff use it to guide what they do.

No matter how well prepared and reported, a strategic plan will not work until its values and content are communicated and enforced throughout the agency. The agency's key managers collectively represent the most effective channel of communication. A constructive, consistent, personal involvement by managers will assure staff at all levels that a sense of purpose exists within the agency.

When strategic planning is first implemented, the agency should begin by clarifying its central mission, using information gained from environmental assessments. Next, the agency should follow a sequence of six interdependent and ongoing steps that enable it to be flexible and responsive to its clients:

1. Establish the agency's mission

2. Develop the goals and objectives of each department

3. Identify the segments of each target audience the agency serves

4. Implement a coordinated action plan to deliver the products and services to the target clients according to specified income and expense budgets

5. Promote the agency, its products, and services in a way that clarifies its image to clients and informs them of how the agency will meet their needs

6. Evaluate progress made toward accomplishing goals and objectives, and use the results to revise the plan

This planning process is central to the marketing model. Vocational rehabilitation agencies already implement most of these steps, but what may be lacking is a coordinated approach that links each of these steps through deliberate staff involvement.

A final consideration must be given to the marketing budget. The marketing department should have its own budget. Budget setting is concluded after action plans are in place because an adequate budget can be prepared only after all the required activities and available resources have been identified.

Implementation:

The implementation of marketing occurs daily after the strategic plan is finished. Marketing functions must be integrated and coordinated with all agency departments so that the client-oriented aspects of the marketing plan pervade the agency.

The agency director must clarify that the primary purpose of marketing is to help the agency and its departments achieve goals and objectives based on client needs. All marketing functions must be viewed as contributors to independence and employment opportunities for persons with disabilities. However, marketing will not supersede services as the major activity of the agency; services are expected to become more effective because of the support from marketing.

Integration of marketing can be encouraged by providing

opportunities for marketing and service staff to work together on joint projects. For example, marketing staff would benefit greatly from the input of staff throughout the agency. Staff workers who are asked to be involved in environmental scanning will recognize the value of such information. To maximize input, staff should be urged to work with marketing personnel to see how their goals and objectives could be enhanced with marketing input. If more supported employment placements are needed, for instance, job development and marketing staff could investigate which employers would be most likely to provide such placements.

Many organizations undertake public relations without implementing the other marketing functions. Although this type of outreach is key to achieving objectives, it must be developed within the context of a *total* marketing effort. All research and planning activities support the effort to market the services of the agency. Too often, marketing is perceived as simply public relations work, such as preparing brochures.

Promotions are intended to help clients familiarize themselves with the agency's resources to meet their needs. For example, the agency may choose a promotional strategy to help employers understand the value of hiring persons with disabilities. There are many different ways to accomplish such a promotion: advertising, public relations, sales, and the use of various media to communicate a message.

The ability to communicate ultimately leads to successful promotions. To communicate effectively, the following principles should be applied:

- Know the needs of clients

- Know what clients are currently doing relative to their needs

- Be able to specify the outcomes that the consumer should achieve

- Be prepared to respond to clients' requests for services

- Design and implement a feedback system that identifies the changes achieved by clients

The message should contain a description of the positive consequences that will occur if the client "buys" the services of the agency. For example, employers are likely to be receptive to a communication if it contains a description of the placement service and its benefits, including how it can reduce their hiring costs.

There are many different ways of communicating. Personal contacts ("sales") are useful with business professionals. Job developers and placement specialists are the agency's primary users of sales techniques. Advertising should be used as well. A combination of paid and public service advertising may be needed because most employers might not hear public service messages when they are announced.

Any contact with the public, and particularly with target audiences, must communicate the purpose and professionalism of the agency. All communications should indicate how prospective employers' needs can be met and should convey a highly credible image of the agency.

Market Research:

One of the most important marketing functions involves formal and informal research to collect pertinent information. Discussions should be held with job developers and placement specialists to assess impressions of employers with high and low potential for hiring people with disabilities. Case files should be reviewed for patterns of jobs in which persons are placed. A study of these patterns could be used to evaluate whether employers recruited by the agency are compatible with agency and consumer goals.

More formal research secures new or more up-to-date information. For example, employers who have hired consumers could be surveyed to determine what future hiring expectations they project and could provide feedback useful for designing new services. Information about past and current placement performance and the level of employers' satisfaction with these efforts serve as an excellent benchmark for specifying goals and objectives for coming years.

To determine their value before being widely implemented, new services should be tested with samples of potential clients. For instance, in testing a new strategy to encourage employers to use the agency's placement services, consumers, employers, and staff could be interviewed for suggested improvements. Knowledge gained from pilot testing typically offsets the research costs by revealing more effective and efficient applications of the agency's services.

Marketing research also aids in the development of a successful promotional strategy. After an agency has decided what message to send to employers, it might wish to convene an employer focus group to gather ideas regarding the best medium and format for delivering the strategy and its message.

CONCLUSION

Understanding how labor markets work equips vocational rehabilitation counselors with a framework for designing services and program management strategies sensitive to the needs of persons with disabilities *and* employers. Applying this framework firmly embeds placement activities within the mission of any rehabilitation agency. Complementing placement services with comprehensive marketing strategies enhances the resources directed at finding employment opportunities for persons with disabilities.

Marketing, as used here, is a philosophy as well as a

process. As a philosophy, it is solidly within the rehabilitation tradition of emphasizing the needs of persons with disabilities. As a process, it coordinates up-to-date techniques to ensure efficient and effective approaches to meeting those needs.

REFERENCES

Bennefield, R. L., & McNeil, J. M. (1989). *Labor force status and other characteristics of persons with a work disability: 1981–1988.* Washington, DC: U.S. Bureau of the Census.

Chun, R. T., & Growick, B. S. (1983). On the congruence of training and placement. *Rehabilitation Counseling Bulletin, 27,* 113–116.

Gilbride, D. D., & Stensrud, R. (1992). Demand-side job: A mode for the 1990s. *Journal of Rehabilitation, 58,* 34–39.

Hester, E. J., & Decelles, P. G. (1985). *The worker who becomes physically disabled: A handbook of incidence and outcomes.* Topeka, KS: The Menninger Foundation.

Kaiser, W. (1983). ATSA. *Rehabilitation Forum, 10,* 20–22.

Louis Harris & Associates. (1986). *The ICD survey of disabled Americans.* New York: Author.

National Institute on Disability and Rehabilitation Research. (1989). Controlling the effects of disability in the workplace. *Rehab Brief, 12*(6).

Rickard, W. H. (1985). *The rehabilitation of long-term disability claimants.* Unpublished monograph.

Roessler, R. T., & Schriner, K. F. (1991). The implications of selected employment concerns for disability policy and rehabilitation practice. *Rehabilitation Counseling Bulletin, 35.*

Tooman, M. L. (1982). Placement of severely disabled persons: Multidiscipline team compared to rehabilitation counselors. *Dissertation Abstracts International, 43,* 2895.

U.S. Bureau of the Census. (1986). *Disability, functional limitations, and health insurance coverage: 1984/85* (Current Population Reports, Series P-70, No. 8). Washington, DC: U.S. Government Printing Office.

Vandergoot, D. (1987). Vocational rehabilitation: current practices and research needs. *Journal of Job Placement, 3,* 21-28.

Vandergoot, D., Staniszewski, S., & Gany, V. (1993). *Employer perceptions of supported workers.* Albertson, NY: National Center for Disability Services. Unpublished manuscript.

Young, J., Rosati, R., & Vandergoot, D. (1986). Initiating a marketing strategy by assessing employer needs for rehabilitation services. *Journal of Rehabilitation, 52,* 37-41.

6

Supported Employment:
An Overview

James Schaller, PhD, Edna Mora Szymanski, PhD, and Cheryl
Hanley-Maxwell, PhD

Dr. Schaller is Assistant Professor, The University of Texas at
Austin. Dr. Szymanski is Professor and Associate Dean, and Dr.
Hanley-Maxwell is Associate Professor and Chair, University of
Wisconsin-Madison, Madison, WI.

KEY POINTS

- Supported employment is a service for people with severe disabilities who otherwise would not be able to obtain or maintain competitive employment. Its core features are competitive employment, integrated settings, the necessity of having a severe disability, and ongoing support.

- Supported employment has become a service delivery option and an employment alternative for persons with severe disabilities. It is especially beneficial for persons with a wide range of disabilities, including chronic mental illness, dual sensory impairment, and traumatic brain injury. Supported employment is potentially applicable for individuals

- with other severe disabilities as well, including cerebral palsy.

- Supported employment developed in the late 1970s and early 1980s as a response to a variety of factors, including the "normalization movement" and trends in special education. These factors are reviewed.

- Supported employment requires an ecological approach to assessment. Such an approach is carried out in two stages: general assessment and an assessment of person-job congruence.

- The authors offer the input-process-output model as a method for increasing the efficacy of supported employment.

INTRODUCTION

Supported employment has become a service delivery option and an employment alternative for people with severe disabilities (Szymanski, Hanley-Maxwell, & Parker, 1988), thereby adding new options for rehabilitation counselors who serve this client population. Although supported employment was initially demonstrated to be a successful option for persons with mental retardation, it has been found to be beneficial for persons with a wide range of disabilities, including chronic mental illness, dual sensory impairment, and traumatic brain injury (Szymanski, Shafer, Danek, & Shiro-Geist, 1990). The purpose of this chapter is to introduce rehabilitation counselors to the supported employment option.

BACKGROUND

Supported employment developed in the late 1970s and early 1980s as a response to a variety of factors, including the normalization movement and trends in special education. A review of these factors can help rehabilitation counselors understand some of the fundamental differences between supported employment and earlier service delivery approaches such as sheltered workshops (Szymanski et al., 1990).

The primary tenet of *normalization* is the delivery of services in environs and with contingencies that are as culturally normal as possible (Rusch & Hughes, 1990). Services that focus on participation and community integration are deemed culturally normal; services that segregate, including employment in a sheltered workshop, are considered abnormal.

As the normalization movement gained momentum, instructional strategies reflected increased emphasis on community-based services and community functioning. In particular, training approaches allowed for more direct entry into the job market (Browder, 1991; Szymanski et al., 1990). The application of behavioral analytic procedures (i.e., applied behavioral analysis) was demonstrated to be highly effective in promoting acquisition, as well as generalization and maintenance, of behaviors and skills (Berg, Wacker, & Flynn, 1990).

Instruction using behavior analytic principles eventually became known as *systematic instruction*. Although it was initially used in educational settings, systematic instruction affected vocational rehabilitation. The improved performance of people with severe disabilities that resulted from application of systematic instruction changed the perceptions of competence for the severely disabled by demonstrating that people could engage in behaviors previously thought to be beyond their ability (Piuma & Udvari-Solner, 1993).

Marc Gold and his colleagues merged systematic instruction and vocational practices, demonstrating that workers with severe disabilities could develop complex assembly skills (Melia, 1990). Other researchers (Rusch & Hughes, 1990) applied similar instructional practices in emerging supported employment programs around the country.

The entry of systematic instruction into rehabilitation was accompanied by a shift in approach from training in a sheltered workshop in preparation for possible placement to placing people in community jobs and then providing training and support services on the job. The latter approach was adopted after research demonstrated people with severe disabilities had difficulties transferring work behaviors from sheltered workshops to community settings (Piuma & Udvari-Solner, 1993). The combination of events described above with trends in special education and rehabilitation paved the way for the development of supported employment (Rehabilitation Act Amendments, 1986).

DEFINITION AND CORE FEATURES

Supported employment is a service for people with severe disabilities who otherwise would not be able to obtain or maintain competitive employment. The core features are competitive employment, integrated settings, the necessity of having a severe disability, and ongoing support. Although early supported employment projects primarily included people with mental retardation, supported employment is potentially applicable for individuals with other severe disabilities including deafness and hearing impairment, blindness and visual impairments, chronic mental illness, traumatic brain injury, and cerebral palsy (Hanley-Maxwell & Szymanski, 1992).

Competitive Employment:

Competitive employment, as it applies to supported employment, is work that is performed on a full-time or part-time basis, averaging at least 20 hours per week of each pay period, for which an individual is compensated in accordance with the Fair Labor Standards Act. The Fair Labor Standards Act allows employers to compensate workers with disabilities with a wage that is (a) lower than the minimum wage; (b) commensurate with those wages paid to other workers with disabilities employed in the same locality and performing the same type, quality, and quantity of work; and (c) is related to the individual's productivity (Wehman, 1989).

Integrated Employment Setting:

Integration of persons with disabilities with persons without disabilities is a key component of supported employment. Various models of supported employment such as the individual placement model, dispersed enclaves, enclaves, and mobile work crew have different amounts of integration. In any model, no more than eight persons with disabilities can work in close proximity to each other. Group models (e.g., mobile work crews, enclaves) are not as desirable as individual placements because they offer less opportunity for interaction with peers, co-workers, and supervisory personnel who do not have disabilities (Federal Register, 1988). In addition, individually appropriate integrated work environments (also known as the *individual placement* model) have greater potential to promote opportunities for work enhancement through learning and performing tasks with increasing difficulty, complexity, and possibly increasing pay, and an overall personalized matching of a worker with a work environment that is complementary, supportive, and enhancing (Brown et al., 1991).

The Necessity of Having a Severe Disability:

The Federal Register (1988) specifies that supported employment is a service for people with severe disabilities who otherwise would be unable to secure employment and remain competitively employed. To be considered eligible for supported employment programs receiving funding under the Rehabilitation Act Amendments, a person must have a disability that seriously limits one or more functional capacities (mobility, communication, self-care, self-direction, interpersonal skills, work tolerance, or work skills) in terms of employability, and can be expected to require multiple vocational rehabilitation services over an extended period of time (Parker, Szymanski, & Hanley-Maxwell, 1989).

Ongoing Support:

A key element of supported employment is the ongoing support that is provided so that persons with severe disabilities can maintain employment. Supported employees must receive ongoing supportive services. Depending on the needs of the supported employee, such services may range from the continued presence of a job coach to job skill training services provided at least twice monthly at the work site.

ECOLOGICAL ASSESSMENT

Supported employment requires an ecological approach to assessment. The term *ecological*, when used in this context, refers to the underlying assumption that people interact with their environments and that both change as a result of the interaction (Parker et al., 1989). Ecological assessment is operationalized in two stages: general assessment and assessment of person-job congruence (Parker et al., 1989).

General Assessment:

Two types of activities are included in general assessment: assessment of the individual and assessment of potential work environments. This information facilitates developing individually appropriate integrated work environments.

Assessment of the Individual

Assessment of the individual involves integrating information from a variety of sources, including school and rehabilitation facility records, interviews with the client and significant others, observation of the performance of job tasks in work settings, and limited use of standardized tests for population description and identification of service needs. This information should assist in answering the following questions:

- What are the client's vocational strengths and weaknesses?

- What are the client's interests and aspirations?

- What training techniques have been most or least successful with this person?

- Has the client received any training in the past? If so, what were the tasks and what prompts or reinforcers were used successfully?

- What types of work settings and job tasks are suitable or unsuitable for this individual?

- Has the client been in enough different work settings and done different job tasks to allow for knowledgeable participation in vocational planning? Is he or she aware of different vocational options, and are those options viable?

- What types of support will this person need in learning the job tasks and related social behaviors for this position?

- What types of contributory support does the client need to adjust to employment (e.g., travel training, money skills, recreational skills, daily living skills)?

- What types of accommodations or adaptations would enhance skill acquisition or performance? (Parker et al., 1989).

Determining preferences and work goals may be difficult with people with severe disabilities. Preferences of the family and individual can provide a starting point for developing a plan to achieve vocational goals. Hagner and Dileo (1994) indicate that stated vocational preferences may not have an occupational name but may be more indicative of a location in the community, a preference for a type of social setting (e.g., a lot of music or noise), or type of physical setting (e.g., outdoor jobs). Hagner and Dileo also caution against dismissing vocational goals that sound unrealistic for an individual with a severe disability because these goals may contain information about how work is perceived and can be incorporated into the individual's life. For example, by ascertaining what aspects of the vocational goal are attractive for the person, it may be possible to discern what parts of the job are meaningful. If a particular social setting, uniform, equipment, or location in the community is especially attractive, this aspect can be used to help identify potential jobs that reflect the individual's preferences.

Answers to these questions should provide the rehabilitation counselor with direction for the initial planning of potential jobs and suitable environments. This information is refined or replaced as new information is learned. Ecological assessment must be an ongoing process as individuals continue to grow and change within their work environments (Parker et al., 1989).

Assessment of Potential Work Environments

Detailed job analyses are used to gather information on potential jobs in the community. Such information is gathered by the rehabilitation counselor or by a job developer to assist with job matches for several persons. Jobs are analyzed for skill requirements, which include work skills, communication, and social skills (Parker et al., 1989). The information obtained by general assessment of the person and job analysis provides the resources for assessing person-job congruence.

Assessment of Person-Job Congruence:

Assessment of person-job congruence involves three steps: (a) identify potential job matches on the basis of comparison of job analyses with the needs and skills of specific persons, (b) identify discrepancies between job/task requirements and individual characteristics and skill acquisition needs, and (c) consider interventions or adaptations to resolve or reduce discrepancies (Piuma & Udvari-Solner, 1993).

Identify Potential Job Matches

Person-job matches are identified by comparing information about the person with the job analyses. Job modification and individual adaptation are options for resolution of potential incompatibilities (Parker et al., 1989). The following conditions need to be met before a match can be considered appropriate:

- The job must be satisfactory to the client

- The job must be a safe one that will not harm the individual or others

- The client's work performance (including interpersonal behaviors) must be satisfactory to the employer

- The job must promote participation in and contribution to the community

- The job must not place undue stress on family supports or limit social supports

- The job must promote individual independence and autonomy (Szymanski et al., 1990)

Identify Discrepancies Between Job/Task Requirements and Individual Characteristics

After potential job matches have been determined, the job analyses are more closely examined for discrepancies between the job requirements and the person's abilities. Job tasks that are likely to present obstacles to successful performance are examined through task analyses (Parker et al., 1989). Cues that occur naturally and are associated with task performance are identified for each step. The resulting task analyses are compared with the individual abilities of the worker. Such comparisons, which are often accomplished through direct observation of the person performing the task, are used to identify discrepancies between the person's attributes and the requirements of the job and to determine interventions.

Piuma and Udvari-Solner (1993) noted that discrepancies may occur in four categories: (a) instructional/individual learning style, (b) environmental, (c) physical/motor sensory, and (d) motivational/behavioral factors. To identify strategies that maximize an individual's ability to work in integrated work environments and to determine if physical adaptations are needed, service providers can systematically select and vary instructional interventions, alter the environment, and modify behavior strategies and materials.

Consider Interventions to Resolve or Reduce Discrepancies

There is a wide range of possible resolutions for discrepancies between individual characteristics and job requirements. Possible resolutions include: (a) individual modifications (e.g., change in appearance, learning compensatory skills), (b) general job modifications (e.g., job restructuring, flexible use of job coach support), and (c) specific task modification (e.g., cue highlighting [highlighting light switch with colored tape], cue substitution [use of a verbal cue instead of an auditory cue], or mediation [use of verbal rehearsal strategies, checklists, or picture prompts]). The following principles should be used to guide the choice and use of resolutions:

- Interventions should be designed to be maximally under the control of the worker, not others.

- Interventions should be designed to facilitate individual autonomy and independence. Use of appropriate training techniques and support services encourages adaptability and independence.

- The least intrusive means that are still effective should be used. Physical prompts, for example, should not be used when a checklist would suffice.

- The most natural interventions for a particular work environment should be used. A pocket reminder list is more natural than a clipboard, and a break in work for early completion of a task is more appropriate than a star on a progress chart or edible reinforcer (Parker et al., 1989).

QUALITY COMPONENTS OF SUPPORTED EMPLOYMENT

In discussing quality dimensions of supported employment,

Szymanski and colleagues (1988) used the input-process-output model to focus on issues relevant to rehabilitation counseling practice. A condensed and updated version of their listing is presented in this section.

Input:

Input components of supported employment are community, individual, and agency resources involved in the delivery of such services. Critical inputs for rehabilitation counselor consideration are consumers, staff, and job sites.

Consumers

Supported employment consumers are workers with severe disabilities. Some persons currently receiving supported employment services may not need ongoing support. Patterson and Curl (1990) suggested that providing supported employment services for people with mild disabilities constitutes an overly intrusive intervention, creates unnecessary and unwarranted dependence, and decreases services available to people with more severe disabilities. In evaluating the quality of supported employment programs, rehabilitation counselors should ask: Does the consumer have a severe disability and does the consumer need ongoing support to remain employed? (Szymanski et al., 1988).

Staff

Considerable progress has been made in the areas of developing and implementing support strategies (Buckley, Mank, & Sandow, 1990), generalizing and maintaining work behaviors (Berg et al., 1990), and teaching social skills on the job (Chadsey-Rusch, 1990). Staff, however, is the key ingredient to the actual implementation of these advances in supported employment practice. In addition to staff knowledge, staff attitudes are also related to the success of supported employees. Currently, staff who are trained or knowledgeable in these areas are far too few in number. It is important to determine if the staff is trained in the necessary techniques and strategies and if staff members hold positive attitudes and expectations for consumers and consumers' work performance (Szymanski et al., 1988).

Job Sites

Quality issues related to job sites and job tasks include diversity of work opportunities, culture of work environments, and integration with co-workers without disabilities. Are job sites diverse and are supported employees placed in job sites according to their interests and skills? Rehabilitation counselors should be wary of programs that use a restricted variety of job sites (Szymanski et al., 1988).

Process:

Process components are activities that define a supported employment program. They include assessment, planning, training, problem solving, and monitoring/documentation.

Assessment

Supported employment interventions should be based on an ecological model of assessment as described in the previous section (Browder, 1991). Standardized instruments, which have not been normed for the special populations for which they are being used, produce inadequate information (Menchetti & Flynn, 1990). To be meaningful, assessment should involve observations of the client in multiple environments, performing a variety of tasks over time, while being instructed or supervised according to training strategies known to be effective. Rehabilitation counselors should consider the following quality questions in evaluating supported employment programs: Is an ecological model used? Are multiple settings and tasks used? If possible, is the assessment longitudinal? Are the assessment instruments or techniques used valid for the population? (Szymanski et al., 1988).

Planning

Supported employment involves carefully matching individual needs and available employment opportunities while providing support to enable effective individual functioning. Careful planning is critical. Rehabilitation counselors should, therefore, consider the following planning-related questions in judging the quality of supported employment programs.

- Is there an individualized match between consumer and job, and is this match based on an analysis of person-environment congruence?

- Is there coordination of — and longitudinal planning for — services with the focus on the needs and resources of the consumer, family, and employer?

- Are there considerations of job modification and restructuring?

- Are funding sources and service providers for ongoing support identified and ensured?

- Does communication exist among all involved parties, including a written plan with specific responsibilities (consumer, service providers, and family), time frames, and criteria for evaluating successful performance?

- Is there coordination between vocational planning and a vocational planning and service delivery (residential and recreational planning and services)?

- Does planning emphasize the least intrusive service delivery to maximize independence, responsibility, and choice-making skills of consumers?

Training

Training procedures are major determinants of successful supported employment outcomes. Effective training strategies are exceedingly important because they promote the acquisition, generalization, and maintenance of work skills and behaviors (Browder, 1991). Indicators of quality training in supported employment programs have suggested the following training-related questions for evaluation of supported employment programs.

- Is training individually determined according to written job and task analysis, and does it include job skills as well as social skills and other work-related behaviors?

- Does training occur primarily at the job site, with supportive training provided at other locations as needed?

- Does training use proven effective strategies for the target population and involve planned generalizations and maintenance of work behaviors with cues and reinforcers identified as naturally occurring and used from the outset?

- Is training organized and systematic, with assistance gradually faded to assist in ensuring stable work performance?

- Do trainers use effective and respectful communication with consumers? (Szymanski et al., 1988).

Problem Solving

Service providers can facilitate consumer performance in integrated work environments through problem solving. The following questions relate to quality problem-solving approaches.

- Are problems and solutions addressed from an ecological perspective, with attention to the environment, relevant interactions, and consumer behavior, or are problems addressed from a deficit orientation, which places the blame for the problem only with the consumer?

- Are resolutions of problems based on a systematic and objective observation and recording of antecedents, behavior, and consequences?

Monitoring/Documentation

The behavioral training strategies used in supported employment rely on systematic monitoring and documentation for effective implementation. Therefore, rehabilitation counselors should consider the following questions in judging the quality of supported employment programs.

- Is service guided by written plans that include short- and long-term goals, behavioral objectives, measurement criteria, and staff responsibility for service delivery and training?

- Is there careful, objective, written documentation of consumer work behavior that includes the level of independence on each task and type of prompts needed for task completion?

- Is evaluation of consumer performance based on consumer goals and job and task analyses?

Output:

The components and activities from the process and input sections combine to produce program output. Benefits to consumers, their families, employers, and communities are the primary output of quality supported employment services. Therefore, rehabilitation counselors should consider the following quality indicators for supported employment outcomes:

- Are consumers and their families satisfied with the job placement and supportive services?

- Are employers satisfied with consumer work performance and agency support services?

- Is there job stability for consumers?

- Do communities benefit from workers with severe disabilities who are integrated throughout the workforce and who produce valued goods and services? (Szymanski et al., 1988).

CONCLUSION

This chapter has provided an overview of the factors that contribute to the development of supported employment, its core features, the meaning of ecological assessment, and quality dimensions. Supported employment provides an effective tool for rehabilitation counselors who wish to increase the employment options for people with severe disabilities. As with any new tool, its ultimate value will depend on its proper use.

REFERENCES

Berg, W. K., Wacker, D. P., & Flynn, T. H. (1990). Teaching generalization and maintenance of work behavior. In F. R. Rusch (Ed.), *Supported employment: Models, methods, and issues.* Chicago: Sycamore.

Browder, D. (1991). *Assessment of individuals with severe disabilities: An applied behavior approach to life skills assessment* (2nd ed.). Baltimore: Brookes.

Brown, L., Udvari-Solner, A., Frattura-Kamshoer, E., Davis, L., Ahlgren, C., Deventer, P., & Jorgensen, J. (1991). Integrated work: A rejection of segregated enclaves and mobile work crews. In L. Meyer, C. Peck, & L. Brown (Eds.), *Critical issues in the lives of people with severe disabilities* (pp. 219-228). Baltimore: Brookes.

Buckley, J., Mank, S., & Sandow, D. (1990). Developing and implementing support strategies. In F. R. Rusch (Ed.), *Supported employment: Models, methods, and issues.* Chicago: Sycamore.

Chadsey-Rusch, J. (1990). Teaching social skills on the job. In F. R. Rusch (Ed.), *Supported employment: Models, methods, and issues.* Chicago: Sycamore.

Federal Register (1988, May 12). Rules and regulations, Part 361 D, the state vocational rehabilitation services program, 53(92), 16982-16986.

Hagner, D., & Dileo, D. (1994). *Working together: Workplace culture, supported employment, and persons with disabilities.* Cambridge, MA: Brookline Books.

Hanley-Maxwell C., & Szymanski, E. (1992). School-to-work transition and supported employment. In R. Parker & E. Szymanski (Eds.), *Rehabilitation counseling: Basics and beyond* (2nd ed., pp. 135-163). Austin: Pro-Ed.

Mank, D. (1994). The underachievement of supported employment: A call for reinvestment. *Journal of Disability Policy Studies, 5*(2), 42-60.

Melia, R. (1990). Introduction. In F. R. Rusch (Ed.), *Supported employment: Models, methods, and issues* (pp. 1-3). Chicago: Sycamore.

Menchetti, B. M., & Flynn, C. C. (1990). Vocational evaluation. In F. R. Rusch (Ed.), *Supported employment: Models, methods, and issues.* Sycamore, Chicago.

Parker, R. M., Szymanski, E. M., & Hanley-Maxwell, C. (1989). Ecological assessment in supported employment. *Journal of Applied Rehabilitation Counseling, 20*(3), 26-33.

Patterson, J. B., & Curl, R. M. (1990). Ethics education. *Rehabilitation Education, 4*, 247-259.

Piuma, F., & Udvari-Solner, A. (1993). *Materials and process manual: Developing low cost vocational adaptations for individuals with severe disabilities.* Madison, WI: University of Wisconsin, Madison.

Rehabilitation Act Amendments of 1986. 29 U.S.C., 701.

Rusch, F. R., & Hughes, C. (1990). Historical overview of supported employment. In F. R. Rusch (Ed.), *Supported employment: Models, methods, and issues.* Chicago: Sycamore.

Szymanski, E. M., Hanley-Maxwell, C., & Parker, R. M. (1988). Quality dimensions of supported employment: A guide for rehabilitation educators. *Rehabilitation Education, 2*, 75-84.

Szymanski, E. M., & Parker, R. M. (1989). Rehabilitation counseling in supported employment. *Journal of Applied Rehabilitation Counseling, 20*(3), 68-69.

Szymanski, E. M., Shafer, M., Danek, M., & Shiro-Geist, C. (1990). Supported employment in rehabilitation education. *Rehabilitation Education, 4*, 233-246.

Wehman, P. (1989). Supported employment: Toward zero exclusion of persons with severe disabilities. In P. Wehman & M. Moon (Eds.), *Vocational rehabilitation and supported employment* (pp. 3-14). Baltimore: Brookes.

7

Work Hardening: A Dynamic Process

Rock Weldon, MA, CVE, CCM, and Gary L. Sigmon, EdD

Mr. Weldon is Vocational Consultant, Weldon & Associates, Greenville, SC. Dr. Sigmon is Vocational Consultant, Blue Ridge Vocational Services, Boone, NC.

KEY POINTS

- *Work hardening* is defined as the rehabilitation of an injured worker with the goal of improving the worker's physical abilities so that he or she is capable of returning to work.

- Work hardening is one of the fastest growing fields of health care today, being driven directly by the spiraling cost of workers' compensation and new federal legislation such as the Americans with Disabilities Act.

- Work hardening programs can trace their history back to the early work of occupational therapists and the "work cure" movement of World War I.

- When an injured worker remains out of the workforce for an extended period of time, he or she develops a "patient personality."

The ultimate goal of work hardening programs is to support the metamorphosis from the "patient personality" to the "worker personality" to facilitate timely return to work.

- Work hardening programs are diverse; they often reflect the needs of a particular community or the personalities and strengths of the professionals involved in the treatment process. The rehabilitation specialist looking for an appropriate program should have specific clients goals in mind and look for specific services from the program.

- The models of work hardening programs discussed in this chapter are: the sports medicine/exercise model, the work activity model, and the integrated vocational or interdisciplinary model.

INTRODUCTION

Work hardening is generally described as the rehabilitation of injured workers with the goal of improving their physical abilities so that they are capable of returning to work. Work hardening may also be known as *work conditioning, work therapy, transition work programs,* or other similar names. As a service, work hardening is one of the fastest growing fields of health care today, being driven directly by the spiraling cost of workers' compensation and new federal legislation such as the Americans with Disabilities Act (ADA) (Key, 1992).

Work hardening programs are rooted in the early work of occupational therapists and the "work cure" movement of World War I. Craft activities were originally adopted to help select appropriate training for patients. The more scientifically based medical community influenced occupational therapists to embrace "work therapy" as it is regarded in the private sector.

Occupational therapists established work evaluation programs using competitive work activities and specific work samples. Reliability of instruments was improved, and formalized reports matched evaluated skills to job skills from the *Dictionary of Occupational Titles* (Harvey-Krefting, 1985).

The Vocational Rehabilitation Act of 1920 and its amendments in 1943 and 1954 increased funding for vocational programs and included those persons in need of physical restoration among its population. Matheson, Ogden, and Violette (1985) note that these expanded opportunities brought about the occupational and curative workshops of the 1940s and 1950s. These workshops used graded activities to improve function and used the patient's job demands as guidelines.

Early program models for formal work hardening and evaluation began in medical physical rehabilitation centers to develop a stronger professional identity (Matheson, 1985). These programs, documented by Worchel (1983), Stevens (1950), and Ayers (1954), first used the now popular multidisciplinary team approach.

Work hardening models of the 1980s and 1990s continue to promote the multidisciplinary approach, but with better defined programs and goals. Indeed, the early efforts of pioneers such as Len Matheson and Keith Blankenship are reflected in many of today's programs. Expanding need has dictated the addition of new professionals such as exercise physiologists, job coaches, and engineers.

DEFINITION

Work hardening programs are as diverse as the many different settings in which they are offered. Likewise, the programs are as complex as the kinds of injuries and types of employment that are often present in the community. Work hardening programs often reflect the needs of a particular community or the personalities and strengths of the professionals involved in the treatment process. Obviously, programs vary greatly from city to city and state to state. In general, however, work hardening programs should be individualized and should address the client's particular problem as it relates to returning to gainful work activities.

Matheson (1985, p. 2) defines *work hardening* as "an individualized work oriented treatment process involving the client in simulated or actual work tasks that are structured and graded to progressively increase tolerances, stamina, endurance, and productivity with the eventual goal of improved employability." The Vocational Evaluation and Work Adjustment Association (1988) has adopted this definition and refers to it in its *VEWAA Glossary*. The Commission on Accreditation of Rehabilitation Facilities (CARF; 1991) has expanded this definition somewhat; the CARF definition appears as follows in *Standards Manual for Organizations Serving People with Disabilities*:

Work hardening programs, which are interdisciplinary in nature, use conditioning tasks that are graded to progressively improve the biomechanical, neuromuscular, cardiovascular/

metabolic, and psychosocial functioning of the person served in conjunction with real or simulated work activities. Work hardening provides a transition between acute care and return to work while addressing the issues of productivity, safety, physical tolerances and worker behaviors. Work hardening is a highly structured, goal oriented, individualized, treatment program designed to maximize the person's ability to return to work. (p. 73)

Although the CARF definition is somewhat longer, there are several areas in which both definitions agree. First, the work hardening program should be highly individualized and designed to meet the needs of each client's particular situation. Second, simulated or actual work tasks should be involved in this process and structured and graded so that the client's tolerances, stamina, and endurance will be progressively increased to the point where he or she will be employable again. Obviously, depending on the extent of the initial injury, each client will require different amounts of time in the work hardening programs.

Table 7.1 identifies the characteristics often associated with the "worker personality" as opposed to the traditional "patient personality" that develops when an injured worker remains out of the workforce for an extended period of time (Brandon, 1987). The ultimate goal of a work hardening program is to support the metamorphosis from the "patient personality" to the "worker personality" to facilitate timely return to work.

These definitions of work hardening emphasize the importance of work-like settings, as well as the expectations and mind set of the worker. Reestablishing the "worker personality" should be a critical part of the process that has often been overlooked by traditional medical models and treatment facilities. By approaching the client as a worker and creating an environment that fosters trust and understanding, the unique needs of each injured worker can be identified and resolved effectively.

Table 7.1

PATIENT PERSONALITY CHARACTERISTICS VERSUS WORKER
PERSONALITY CHARACTERISTICS

Patient Personality

- All supervision is considered criticism
- Not willing to meet employer time demands
- Co-workers viewed suspiciously
- Unmotivated and indifferent to achievement of goals
- Cannot focus on a specific goal other than health
- Blames all problems on outside forces
- Becomes focused unproductively on the injury
- Becomes injury dependent—search for total cure
- Looking for a financial windfall to solve all problems
- Becomes alcohol or drug dependent
- Wanders aimlessly through the day
- Turns life over to outside influences
- Refuses to compromise or alter behavior
- Ignores safety steps during services
- Overreacts or underreacts emotionally

Worker Personality

- Willing to accept supervision
- Willing to adhere to work schedule
- Willing to participate with co-workers
- Able to pay attention to detail
- Able to set realistic goals (both short- and long-term)
- Able to accept personal responsibility
- Able to place injury-related problems into perspective
- Able to recognize limits
- Able to manage financial resources
- Able to avoid alcohol and drug dependency
- Able to manage personal time
- Able to manage outside influences
- Attempts to follow corrective instructions
- Demonstrates caution, but will attempt activity
- Demonstrates full range of emotion

Source: Brandon, T. (1987). *ERGOS work simulator training seminar
manual.* Tucson: Work Recovery Centers.

WORK HARDENING MODELS

Work hardening programs exist in a variety of configurations and settings, but in general seem to follow the orientation of the staff involved in the treatment process. Programs can range in complexity from basic exercise to comprehensive multidisciplinary programs. It can be expected that a more complicated rehabilitation case will require a more complex program to meet the client's needs.

Models discussed in this chapter include the sports medicine/exercise model, the work activity model, and the integrated vocational or interdisciplinary model. For purposes of this discussion, these models progress in complexity and comprehensiveness as well as increased involvement of various disciplines.

Sports Medicine/Exercise Model:

Typically, sports medicine programs, staffed by physical therapists, tend to be based in a hospital as an extension of a physical therapy department or operated as an extension to acute rehabilitation service in a private clinic. Therapists in this type of program establish goals to increase mobility, strength, and self-confidence. Program activities include stretching and general body conditioning with special attention paid to the injured area of the body. Specialized body building equipment, such as the Nautilus, NordicTrack, Mini-Gym, or Cybex, may be used in this process. Other traditional equipment (weights, treadmills, exercycles, and barbells) are also common. Work-related activities involve materials such as bricks, concrete blocks, hand trucks, wheelbarrows, and possibly crates that are lifted to predetermined shelf heights.

A program at this level is most useful in uncomplicated cases, when the main problem facing an injured worker is physical conditioning secondary to an illness or injury. The highly motivated client will most likely benefit from this type of aggressive rehabilitation program.

A typical day in this type of program includes stretching; strengthening exercises; and exercises to increase tolerance and stamina using exercycles, treadmills, or aquatic exercises. In addition, these programs involve instruction in correct body mechanics, posture, anatomy, physiology, and other topics that might foster a general understanding of the injury.

Work hardening programs that use a sports medicine/ exercise approach adopt the philosophy and goals of the sports trainer: to allow the injured athlete to function and to get him or her back to 100% performance as soon as possible. To accomplish these goals, the injured athlete begins passive exercise/therapy immediately following the injury (assuming medical feasibility) progressing to active, resistive, exercise, and muscle restrengthening.

Work Activity Model:

Building on the sports medicine/exercise model is the work activity model. This model includes the general conditioning and exercise approaches of the sports medicine/exercise model in addition to more in-depth work simulation activities. Work simulation activities should represent the actual jobs or industries indicated by the job goal for the client. The job simulation activities can either replicate the actual tools and materials the worker has used in past work or simply replicate the biomechanical movements necessary to perform past work or job goals of the client. These work simulation activities may be built by the center's personnel or purchased through commercial work sample/work simulation manufacturers. In this model, a variety of rehabilitation specialists may be used in addition to physical therapists, including occupational therapists, vocational specialists, rehabilitation engineers, and exercise physiologists.

Moreover, it may be determined through the use of on-site (ergonomic) job analysis that a client may not possess the ability or physical capacity to return to his or her previous occupation. In this case, the staff (occupational therapist, vocational evaluator) may perform vocational testing and/or transferability of skills analysis to identify feasible occupational goals. Vocational testing also may be used to measure a person's vocational aptitude, educational skills, vocational interest, temperaments (personality variables), and cognitive abilities.

A typical day in this type of program begins with stretching and strengthening activities, followed by carefully selected work simulation activities designed gradually to build work tolerance consistent with the job goal. Participants also are involved in instructional programs aimed at increasing their understanding of proper body mechanics, occupational safety, and injury prevention.

Participants in this work activity model have greater needs than those in a sports medicine/exercise program. It should be expected that clients in these programs may be involved on a 3–5-day per week program for a longer period of time as indicated by the nature and severity of the injury. Total program length at this level depends on the severity of the injury.

Integrated Vocational/Interdisciplinary Model:

For the more complex rehabilitation case involving complicated issues or extended length of disability, an integrated vocational/interdisciplinary model as described by CARF is the most appropriate. This model includes all of the approaches to service delivery of the previous models and may also incorporate psychological services, job development/placement services, dietary-nutritional counseling, substance abuse counseling and industrial engineering/rehabilitation engineering. Table 7.2 outlines a sample daily schedule.

To receive CARF accreditation, a program must adhere to the following standards:

The interdisciplinary team should be made up of the following professionals: Occupational Therapist, Physical Therapist, Psychologist, Vocational Specialist. Based upon the needs of the individual, the following services should be made available:

Alcohol and drug counseling, dietary services, exercise physiology, industrial/rehabilitation engineering, orthotics and prosthetics, academic remediation, and social services. (Commission on Accreditation of Rehabilitation Facilities, 1991, pp. 74–75)

Table 7.2
SAMPLE DAILY SCHEDULE FOR
INTERDISCIPLINARY/VOCATIONAL MODEL

8:30–9:15 AM	Warm-up; walk
9:15–9:30	Break
9:30–10:00	Everyday strength exercises
10:00–10:45	Stretch
10:45–11:15	Individual/group counseling
11:15 –12:00 PM	Educational session
12:00–1:00	Lunch
1:00–2:00	Work hardening
2:00–2:15	Break
2:15–3:45	Work hardening
3:45–4:15	Relaxation techniques
4:15–4:30	Clean-up

This model should be comprehensive enough to meet the total needs of the injured worker by addressing the issues preventing the emergence of the worker personality and flexible enough to address the specific needs of each individual who enters the program.

PROCESS

To address specific needs, realistic attainable vocational goals must be determined for each client before the implementation of a work hardening program. The process begins with a thorough review of the medical record, determination of the clients' current activity level, and work history review.

Physical testing begins with the determination of physical attributes; that is, height, weight, body fat composition, cardiovascular fitness, and range of motion. Performance testing should be completed to measure the client's ability to meet the physical demands of work as defined by the U.S. Department of Labor. These variables include lifting, carrying, pushing and pulling capacity, climbing, balancing, stooping, kneeling, crouching, crawling, reaching, handling, fingering, feeling, hearing, seeing, and speaking. Also, endurance factors relative to the client's sitting, standing, and walking tolerance should be assessed.

Based on findings of this initial evaluation and the results of a functional capacity evaluation, a prescriptive individualized work hardening program is developed for the client. This plan addresses the physical needs and other services required by the client to return to work consistent with the defined job goal.

Ongoing evaluation of the client's progress is necessary to monitor appropriateness of the job goal. Program modifications may be necessary if an alternative job goal is deemed necessary. This is usually accomplished by weekly staffings. Staffings are held so that each member of the rehabilitation team can discuss the progress being made by the client. Should an alternative job goal become necessary, the team has all the information necessary to implement the needed changes.

WORK HARDENING PROGRAM SELECTION

Work hardening programs vary greatly. The rehabilitation specialist looking for an appropriate work hardening program should have specific client goals in mind. Also, he or she should look for specific services from the program that is ultimately chosen.

Qualified Staff:

Staff members have degrees in occupational therapy, physical therapy, exercise physiology, or vocational specialties. Training in areas of anatomy, physiology, testing, exercise, occupational information, and other medical and psychological aspects of disability should be expected. Staff members should possess professional certificates or licenses in their appropriate fields. Additional training and experience in the areas of work hardening, functional capacity evaluation, job analysis, vocational evaluation, and job modification are often beneficial. Manufacturers of equipment for evaluation and treatment may also offer training or certification in the use and interpretation of their specific equipment.

Timely Information:

The rehabilitation specialist should expect weekly or bi-weekly reports on the progress of the client. This information should include objective measurable information by which progress (or lack thereof) can be measured. Problems or changes in program goals should be discussed on a timely basis with the specialist. This is often accomplished by including the specialist in weekly staffings.

Computerized Testing:

Many programs are using computer-assisted treatment or evaluation equipment. Such methods should be closely scrutinized, but generally they can provide additional information. Consistency of efforts using the coefficient of variation as well as objective, repeatable information can be obtained. Computers often record testing or treatment data as it is being generated, thus reducing the possibility of errors. Computers may also be used to administer testing and to produce standardized protocols.

Work-Specific Results:

Outcomes from a work hardening program should include specific information concerning a client's ability to perform competitive work activities. Job titles and codes from the *Dictionary of Occupational Titles* accompanied by appropriate physical demands are desirable.

Standards such as those used by industrial engineers (e.g., methods time measurement) can provide additional information concerning a client's ability to perform work competitively and productively.

CONCLUSION

Work hardening is a multidisciplinary treatment modality with the purpose of assisting persons to achieve a level of productivity that is acceptable in the competitive labor market (May, 1988).

The various models presented in this chapter demonstrate the dynamic nature of work hardening. As we face new challenges, such as those imposed by the ADA, work hardening programs will continue to be important tools in assisting employers as they seek to create safe and productive work environments.

REFERENCES

Ayers, A. J. (1954). A form used to evaluate the work behavior of patients. *American Journal of Occupational Therapy, 8,* 73–74.

Brandon, T. (1987). *ERGOS work simulator training seminar manual.* Tucson: Work Recovery Centers.

Commission on Accreditation of Rehabilitation Facilities. (1992). *Standards manual for organizations serving people with disabilities.* Tucson: Author.

Harvey-Krefting, L. (1985). The concept of work in occupational therapy: A historical review. *American Journal of Occupational Therapy, 39,* 301–307.

Key, G. L. (1992). Work hardening—a marketplace definition. (1992). *Rehabilitation Therapy Products Review, Nov/ Dec,* 26–27.

Matheson, L. (1985). *Work capacity evaluation: An interdisciplinary approach to industrial rehabilitation.* Anaheim, CA: Employment and Rehabilitation Institute of California.

Matheson, L., Ogden, L., & Violette, K. (1985). Work hardening: Occupational therapy in industrial rehabilitation. *American Journal of Occupational Therapy, 39,* 301–307.

May, V., III. (1988). Work hardening and work capacity evaluation: definition and process. *Vocational Evaluation and Work Adjustment Bulletin, 21,* 61.

Stevens, A. (1950). Work evaluations in rehabilitation. *Occupational Therapy in Rehabilitation, 29,* 157–161.

Vocational Evaluation and Work Adjustment Association. (1988). *VEWAA glossary.* Menomonie, WI: University of Wisconsin-Stout, Materials Development Center.

Worchel, P. (1983). Program for industrial therapy. *American Journal of Occupational Therapy, 17,* 117–122.

8

Vocational Evaluation of Clients with Traumatic Brain Injury

Robert T. Fraser, PhD, CRC

Dr. Fraser is Professor in the Department of Neurology, with joint appointments in Neurological Surgery and Rehabilitation Medicine, University of Washington; and Consultant, Associates in Rehabilitation and Neuropsychology, Seattle, WA.

KEY POINTS

- Vocational evaluation of clients with traumatic brain injury (TBI) requires individualized planning, varied procedures in actual job situations, and repeated evaluations. Several kinds of evaluations are needed for clients with more severe TBI injuries.

- The Americans with Disabilities Act requires the provision of a vocationally comprehensive and environmentally relevant assessment of clients with TBI.

- Three levels of vocational assessment are used for clients with TBI: specialized return to work/ transferable skills assessment, basic/short-term evaluation, and intermediate evaluation.

- The first level of evaluation involves conducting a comprehensive interview and a review of pertinent background information, medical records, and serial testing results.

- The basic or short-term evaluation includes neuropsychological testing, vocational interest assessment, personality functioning assessment, work values identification, and academic achievement testing.

- The intermediate level is used to ascertain a client's capacity to return to a prior job, reenter work in a position in which transferable skills can be used, or perform in an entirely new job area identified in the basic evaluation.

INTRODUCTION

Vocational evaluation aims to accomplish two primary goals: (a) the accurate assessment of clients' competence relative to their vocational assets and limitations, and (b) the attainment of a prognosis relative to performance success in competitive work environments (Nadolsky, 1985). In addition to testing, the rehabilitation process involves a comprehensive overview of available background information. Real or simulated work activities are used systematically as a basis for assessment and, to some degree, for vocational exploration.

With the advent of Title I of the Americans with Disabilities Act in July of 1992, the need to use environmentally relevant performance criteria, as related to the essential functions of a job, has become even more critical. As the severity of traumatic brain injury (TBI) increases, using environmentally relevant stimuli in vocational assessment enables vocational counselors to tap into the client's learning capacities. Accordingly, vocational counselors should afford the client every opportunity to demonstrate capabilities suitable to a vocation.

Vocational evaluation of a client with TBI "is a different process than that used with other disabled populations. Effective vocational evaluation requires individualized planning, flexible and varied procedures in actual/realistic job situations, and repeated evaluations over time and under varying conditions" (McMahon, 1986, p. 131). This type of evaluation involves a client-environment interaction that includes not only the specific work activity at hand but also the learning cues provided from the larger work setting.

A number of general guidelines can be used in the vocational evaluation of clients with TBI. For instance, short, 1-day evaluations and brief transferable skills assessments often are not useful for clients with moderate-to-severe brain injuries. Most of these clients require a longer-term evaluation, involving several weeks, to determine whether several months of intermediate-level evaluation are needed before the choice of a job placement approach. The approach to moving TBI clients as quickly as possible to relevant work sampling or in vivo work evaluation activities should be relatively economical.

Vocational evaluation procedures for clients with TBI: (a) require more time to establish whether clients can perform a task (due to difficulties with both cognitive functioning and motor slowing), (b) must emphasize how clients can best learn to perform a task, and (c) must focus on an individualized assessment approach that avoids testing clients in groups. It is helpful to administer tests at different times of the day for several days to determine periods of stronger or weaker performance.

OBTAIN ADEQUATE BACKGROUND INFORMATION

Three levels of vocational assessment are generally used for clients with TBI:

1. Specialized return to work/transferable skills assessment

2. Basic or short-term evaluation

3. Intermediate level of evaluation (usually lasting several months)

The backbone of these assessment interventions involves a comprehensive interview and review of all available pertinent information. According to the Vocational Evaluation and Work Adjustment Association (1975), this would consist of screening and clinical case studies.

A review of background information includes a study of basic identifying information, education, prior work history, avocational activity, military background, family's educational and vocational history, a history of emotional functioning and life events within the family, assessment of available social support (e.g., emotional, operational, and information provision) by family members and significant others in the community, and a comprehensive review of medical records.

Medical records are reviewed to identify the severity of the disability by time spent in a coma, Glasgow Coma (Teasdale & Jennett, 1974) or Rancho Scale scores (Duncan, 1990), length of posttraumatic amnesia, description of postinjury hemorrhaging, periods of disorientation, behavioral outbursts, and other similar information. It is particularly important to review summary reports by members of the allied health team and include these reports in the final discharge summaries after acute and postacute care (if available).

As presented through serial testing results, neuropsychological functioning also should be studied carefully. It is particularly important to identify preinjury emotional or personality disorders as well as any history of substance abuse. Although there is often a considerable period of postinjury abstinence, substance abuse tends to increase for many survivors for approximately 1 year after the injury.

When interviewing clients, it is important to identify their exact amount and source of financial support, specific salary requirements for returning to work, any litigation that might interfere with the planning of a rehabilitation plan, and the perspective and desires of family members or significant others pertinent to the client's decision to return to work. These issues must be clarified and related interventions agreed on *prior to* intensive evaluation and rehabilitation efforts. In most cases, the client, family members, and the rehabilitation agency representative commit to a plan *in writing* to avoid a misunderstanding or miscommunication. This is particularly important when psychopathology is evident in the client, the client's spouse, family member(s), or significant others.

ASSESSMENT OF SPECIALIZED RETURN-TO-WORK AND TRANSFERABLE SKILLS

Clients with extensive backgrounds related to a specific job generally do not enter an open-ended type of evaluation; rather, they are evaluated relative to their specialized prior job skills, especially those that are transferable. Initially, this may involve a job analysis at the task level of specificity with regard to a prior job and include information on all the established criteria for performing the job successfully.

Specialized assessment must determine a client's ability to return to prior work. Is additional training necessary? Does some type of reasonable accommodation have to be implemented to include a procedural modification in the work activity? Do physical changes need to be made at the job site? Will the client need to use some type of adaptive equipment? A procedural adaptation may involve changes in shifts, a co-worker assisting with some nonessential parts of the job, or short-term job coaching or co-worker mentoring/training.

In a number of cases, a client's ability to return to a former occupation after suffering TBI cannot be determined with a few weeks' worth of specialized assessment. In these cases, the client must be evaluated on an intermediate level. This may involve several months of in vivo job site training by a specialized trainer, job coach, or co-worker. Useful data are gathered relative to productivity and accuracy of performance. This helps to determine whether return to work is viable. When the client is unable to return to work at a full-performance level, such data can be used to identify whether the employer would accept an on-the-job training or some other type of subsidy to return the client to full-time employment on a graduated basis. Some employers might be receptive to a U.S. Department of Labor "selective worker certification" status, in which the client is paid a lesser wage tied to actual productivity on the job.

Physical modifications to a job site or the use of adaptive equipment can be evaluated through the consultation services of a technologist or rehabilitation engineer, an occupational therapist, or, at times, a physical therapist (if a rehabilitation counselor or job coach requires assistance). The Job Accommodation Network (JAN) (1995) at West Virginia University also can be contacted with regard to specific accommodation recommendations.

If it is determined that a TBI client cannot return to a prior job, it may be helpful to use computer searches to identify positions in which prior work skills can be utilized (*OASYS,* 1983; *The CAPCO Connection,* 1995). In some cases, these skills can be pinpointed by examining the client's work history; in other cases, companies offering jobs that require the client's residual capabilities must be located.

BASIC OR SHORT-TERM EVALUATION

If a transferable job goal cannot be identified readily, the client is best served by a basic or short-term evaluation to establish potential new goals. Basic or short-term evaluation is the cornerstone to the work access (or return-to-work effort), particularly with clients who have no substantial work history or clients who require the establishment of new job goal(s).

In addition to a comprehensive review of existing background information on current or prior treatments by allied health team members and a thorough clinical interview (often including discussions with family members and significant others), the core components to the short-term evaluation include neuropsychological testing, vocational interest assessment, emotional/personality functioning assessment, work values/reinforcers identification, academic achievement testing, or specific vocational aptitude and work sample system evaluation. Complete information regarding the client's physical functioning must be available; if this information is not available, a physical capacities evaluation must be obtained (particularly for clients with prior severe orthopedic injuries). Several screening inventories are helpful in assessing physical functioning or independent living capacities (e.g., the Consumer Employment Screening Form or the Revised Consumer Employment Screening Form); however, a comprehensive evaluation is usually the most beneficial way to determine the client's physical capacities (Thomas, 1990).

Neuropsychological Testing:

Neuropsychological testing assesses a broad range of cognitive abilities, including attention and concentration, sensory-motor abilities, language abilities, memory capacities, visuospatial skills, problem-solving and abstract-reasoning abilities, and general cognitive efficiency. Typical batteries include the Halstead-Reitan Neuropsychological Test Battery (Reitan & Wolfson, 1985), the Luria-Nebraska Neuropsychological Battery (Golden, Hammeke, & Purisch, 1980), and others that are more individually tailored to the perceived difficulties of the client (Reitan & Wolfson, 1985).

To attain expertise in evaluating the working capabilities and labor market potential of TBI clients, rehabilitation counselors should be familiar with the core neuropsychological tests in this area. The Wechsler Adult Intelligence Scale-Revised (WAIS-R) generally is administered as a standard component of an assessment of work-related capacities and labor market potential (Wechsler, 1981). In some instances, the McCarron-Dial Work Evaluation System, a battery of neurometric and behavioral measures, is used in place of other standard neuropsychological batteries (McCarron & Dial, 1976). This system tends to add valuable information to that secured from a standard battery; however, it is helpful when used alone if no other neuropsychological test results are available.

Neuropsychological test results should be made available as soon as possible (even if they take the form of a brief checklist). Delays in receipt of this information disrupt rehabilitation planning and inhibit the value of the entire vocational evaluation process. A recent monograph by Uomoto (1991) reviewed the use of neuropsychological testing in vocational rehabilitation planning. If comprehensive neuropsychological testing is available (particularly at 1 or more years from the time of injury), additional testing may not be necessary. Even though neuropsychological testing sometimes overestimates or underestimates actual job performance, it still provides a solid base for setting goals and anticipating accommodation or compensatory strategies.

Vocational Interest Assessment:

Standard vocational interest inventories, such as the Career Assessment Inventory, the Strong Vocational Interest Inventory (more professionally oriented), the Gordon Occupational Checklist II (Gordon, 1981), or reading-free inventories (e.g., the Reading-Free Vocational Interest Inventory or the Valpar Guide to Occupational Exploration) are the most widely used for assessing the vocational interests of TBI clients. The Gordon Occupational Checklist II is helpful because it is task specific, involves a wide range of "blue collar" semiskilled and skilled work activities, and includes career goal questions. The questions provide the counselor with helpful writing samples and indices of the cogency of the client's thinking or executive functioning.

Emotional/Personality Functioning:

Information regarding emotional/personality functioning can be gathered through structured psychiatric interviews, the Minnesota Multiphasic Personality Inventories I and II, or the Millon Clinical Multiaxial Inventories I–III (Millon, 1994). This information can help counselors better understand the client's emotional status and plan his or her entry or reentry into the workforce accordingly.

The Millon Clinical Multiaxial Inventories assess characterologic structure — although there is often a narcissistic scale elevation due to the cognitive effects of TBI (i.e., a self-centeredness). These inventories are interpreted by psychologists and can be administered with neuropsychological batteries. For clients with no known prior psychopathology, the Sixteen Personality Factor Questionnaire (Institute for Personality and Ability Testing, 1991) can be of assistance in vocational planning. To further understand behavioral issues, the Worker Performance Assessment (Roessler, 1988), developed at the Arkansas Research and Training Center, can be used to evaluate a client's work and interpersonal behaviors while involved in group or task activities.

Work Values/Reinforcers:

Many survivors of TBI are young men in their late teens or early twenties whose vocational interests are not clear-cut at the time of injury. Consequently, "things about work" (e.g., salary level, outdoor activity, the opportunity to work with a group of young men or women, or an aesthetically pleasing environment) may be more important than the work activity itself to these clients. Much of the information about contextual reinforcers for working can be established through interviewing the client and family or significant others. Some standard inventories, such as the Career Value Scale (1987), also may be of assistance in establishing a set of values that the client considers worth reinforcing. Unless these values can be established, particularly with young adults, the client will not sufficiently engage in the vocational entry or reentry process.

Academic Achievement:

Academic achievement testing typically involves the use of tests such as the Wide Range Achievement Test (WRAT) (which is often given as a complement to the neuropsychological testing battery), the Peabody Individual Achievement Test (PIAT), and the Adult Basic Learning Examination (Choppa, 1992). The WRAT is a screening inventory; the PIAT is for clients who are disadvantaged and do not speak English (it is administered orally in approximately 40 minutes). The Adult Basic Learning Examination is comprehensive, involves up to 3 hours of administration, and contains 5 subtests (vocabulary, reading, spelling, number operations, and problem solving). The Adult Basic Learning Examination is designed specifically for adults involved in job training and adult education programs.

Vocational Aptitudes:

A number of vocational aptitude batteries are available: the McCarron-Dial Work Evaluation System (McCarron & Dial,

1976), Vocational Transit, and the Differential Aptitude Test. Because the McCarron-Dial Work Evaluation System is sensitive to brain impairment, it frequently is used at vocational evaluation centers that treat TBI clients. Other vocational aptitude tests — the Bennett Mechanical Comprehension Test or the Crawford Small Parts Dexterity Tests — are available for assessing specific aptitudes. However, if the evaluator focuses on a specific ability, it is more useful and valid to use an actual work sample drawn from a targeted position and job activity versus attempting to infer specific ability as a function of performance based on a commercially available test.

Work Sample Systems:

The use of work samples can be of assistance — particularly when the counselor is searching for "some" postinjury residual ability that complements client interests; if this can be identified, the counselor can further clarify suitable and realistic job goals for the client. Botterbusch (1992) and Weed and Field (1990) have reviewed work sample systems; they emphasized psychomotor and visuospatial skills versus verbal ability. In most cases, commercially available systems are bypassed if actual work activity or a work sample directly related to the job goal can be secured.

An Integrative Summary:

A vocational evaluation of TBI clients should include all available relevant information from other allied health specialties (particularly neuropsychologists, speech and language pathologists, and physical therapists) (Fraser, 1991). The summary should specify:

- Job goals and the choice of a placement approach (when possible)

- Barriers that require intervention and types of potential accommodation

- Presence of the need for longer-term, intermediate assessment before a placement approach can be chosen

- Degree of need for continued vocational exploration

- Types of avocational or volunteer activities that might be useful in improving the client's quality of life (if a client is not a candidate for competitive placement)

If formal job-related training is indicated, it should be specified, with any accommodation that might be helpful. As discussed by Thomas in Chapter 3, the evaluation should summarize functional strengths and potential limitations in relation to the specific job recommendations. This facilitates the development of better methods of "reasonable accommodation" within the context of the essential functions of recommended jobs. Any modification to standard testing involved in the vocational evaluation and its impact on the client's performance also must be noted.

Choice of a Placement Model:

Part of the basic evaluation recommendations should elaborate on the work access/reentry job placement model that will be most useful in stabilizing a client with traumatic brain injury on the job (Fraser, McMahon, & Wehman, 1991). The following factors should be considered carefully when choosing a job placement approach or model:

- The neuropsychological pattern of asset and deficit (including information from actual neuropsychological testing and work sampling)

- The client's current financial salary needs and existing subsidy amounts

- Work-relevant variables (time on the job, job complexity, receptivity of co-workers or supervisors to mentoring)

- The client's current emotional and interpersonal functioning

Some clients who do not have severe injuries simply may require advice about job search strategies. Other clients, particularly those with moderate or severe injuries, may need more basic services (e.g., to be brokered to an employer, receive assistance with job matching to their residual abilities and with job development). Some will need assistance on the job, including some type of reasonable accommodation.

Clients with severe brain injuries or clients with a localized problem, such as significant memory deficit or behavioral difficulty, may require some type of *agency-based support*—one-on-one job coaching, an enclave situation with a job coach, contracted job sharing with a co-worker without disabilities, or paid mentoring (by either a community college instructor or a retired worker). A *natural support* at the work site entails adopting a supervisor or co-worker as a trainer. Sometimes these costs are subsidized through state vocational rehabilitation funding, or an arrangement is made directly with the co-worker or supervisor for salary increments based on the training function (Curl, Fraser, Cook, & Clemmons, 1996). In some cases, a co-worker does not function as a trainer, but does provide some type of physical assistance or may perform a small part of the job for the TBI client whose limitations preclude performing specific job components.

The actual placement model frequently becomes apparent through information gathered at the basic evaluation stage. In other cases, this determination requires assessment throughout the intermediate level of evaluation. Whenever possible, recommendations as to the optimal job placement approach or consideration of several approaches should be included in the evaluation.

INTERMEDIATE EVALUATION

The intermediate level of evaluation is applied to ascertain a client's capacity to return to a prior job, reenter work in a position in which transferable skills can be used, or perform in an entirely new job area as identified in the basic evaluation. In addition to assessing client performance, this level of evaluation also serves the purposes of vocational exploration.

Intermediate evaluation typically lasts 1–4 months; takes place at an actual job site; and involves a collection of specific data relevant to work productivity, work accuracy, and diverse work behaviors necessary for the chosen job goal. Seldom exceeding 5 or 6 months, a placement model normally can be chosen with 1–4 months' worth of data. With increasing time on a job tryout, client dependency can develop in relation to a setting in which financial remuneration is unlikely (Bolton, 1974). These levels of assessment can be established within federal agencies (U.S. Office of Personnel Management, 1982), as volunteer positions within universities (and other nonprofit organizations), or within the private sector under a new U.S. Department of Labor waiver (Bolton, 1974; Curl et al., 1996). Under the new U.S. Department of Labor (1993) waiver, a client cannot try out for more than 215 hours; this would be about 5 weeks full-time, 11 weeks part-time, or 14 weeks at 15 hours a week.

A vocational rehabilitation counselor, vocational evaluator, job coach, or other allied health team member monitors the client's work productivity, accuracy, behavioral performance, and other types of information that must be established. Some clients require job coaching during this period; other clients require a behavioral management plan, which can be established and implemented prior to consideration of a competitive placement. Data are collected daily. Meetings with the supervisor, co-worker/mentor (unpaid or paid), and the rehabilitation counselor or agency representative will occur more often depending on the client's degree of cognitive or behavioral impairment.

As jobs increase in cognitive complexity, a speech patholo-
gist or a neuropsychologist may visit the workplace to recommend compensatory strategies or assist in training the client
(Fraser & Baarslag-Benson, 1994). Assistive technologists, occupational therapists, or physical therapists also might recommend physical modification to the work station or assistive
equipment if recommendations cannot be established through
the JAN. Reasonable accommodations relative to changes in
work procedures (i.e., physical modification of the work station or use of assistive equipment) can be assessed carefully
during the intermediate level of evaluation. A review of accommodation procedures specific to clients with TBI has been
published by Warren (1991).

The primary goal of this intermediate level of evaluation is
to establish whether specific job recommendations, as outlined in the basic evaluation, are feasible. At the end of this
period of assessment, a placement approach is chosen and an
effort made toward competitive employment. In some cases,
targeted formal training or retraining still may be required
before placement efforts.

Certain clients will not have a competitive potential, even
with agency-based or natural supports at the work site and
accommodation efforts. These clients may profit through the
U.S. Department of Labor selective worker certification. Clients who need to maintain their Social Security subsidy may be
able to work on a part-time basis or, through the development
of Plan for Achieving Self-Sufficiency (PASS) or Individual
Work-Related Expenses (IWRE) plans, maintain their Social
Security funding due to the cost of an attendant, transportation, or other work-related expenditures. If clients cannot
work competitively, or can only work part-time, volunteer or
avocational options should be recommended to assist them
with structuring their time and generally improving their life
satisfaction. A therapeutic recreational specialist is helpful in
this area.

CASE STUDY

Ken, a 23-year-old truck driver, suffered a severe TBI (Glasgow Coma Scale score of 8; 4 days in coma) in an auto accident. Alcohol-induced recklessness was suspected but could not be established because he was found some time after the accident. Family information suggested occasional binge drinking. An evaluation of his physical capacities revealed a partial hemiparesis and physical lifting/pulling restrictions that precluded his return to work as a truck driver. He had some experience in the welding field, but a *transferable skill assessment* suggested that he would not perform at an adequate level of eye-hand coordination. He entered a *basic level* of evaluation to establish a new job goal.

After 3–4 weeks, a new job goal of becoming a stock inventory clerk was established. A company for which Ken had worked previously had several open positions in this job category, which had a light-to-medium lifting requirement. He entered an *intermediate level* of evaluation, during which he tried out the new position on a part-time unpaid basis — mornings from 9–12 for 8 weeks. Worker's Compensation coverage was established through his rehabilitation facility. A job coach was used as an *agency-based* support for 2 weeks due to some of Ken's memory deficits.

After a standard protocol was established for Ken's daily activities, he performed at approximately a 65% productivity level at the end of 8 weeks. The company was willing to hire him full-time with an on-the-job training subsidy for 4 months while Ken improved his productivity. A company supervisor subsumed training responsibility from the job coach. Ken successfully completed his on-the-job-training and was hired permanently. The agency rehabilitation counselor followed Ken on a monthly basis for 1 year after placement; Ken continued to perform well and remained abstinent from alcohol.

CONCLUSION

The challenge to the rehabilitation counselor or vocational evaluator involved in the assessment process of clients with TBI is not only to identify specific and reasonable job goals, but also to devise and implement a realistic strategy for achieving them. The right placement model must be chosen, and it must be determined whether reasonable accommodation is required. The Americans with Disabilities Act attaches significant responsibility to the role of the evaluator and the evaluating agency: providing a vocationally comprehensive and environmentally relevant assessment of clients with TBI. In fully accepting this challenge, rehabilitation counselors perform a great service for survivors of TBI who are attempting to enter or reenter the workforce.

REFERENCES

Bolton, B. (1974). *Introduction to rehabilitation research.* Springfield, IL: C. C. Thomas.

Botterbusch, K. F. (1992). Vocational assessment and evaluation systems. In *Vocational evaluation project final report.* Menomonee, WI: University of Wisconsin-Stout, Stout Vocational Rehabilitation Institute, Materials Development Center.

CAPCO Connection. (1995). Spokane, WA: The Capability Corp.

Career value scale. (1987). Jacksonville, FL: Talico.

Choppa, A., et al. (1992). Vocational evaluation in private sector rehabilitation. In *Vocational evaluation project final report.* Menomonee, WI: University of Wisconsin-Stout, Stout Vocational Rehabilitation Institute, Materials Development Center.

Curl, R. C., Fraser, R. T., Cook, R., & Clemmons, D. C. (1996). Traumatic brain injury vocational rehabilitation: Preliminary findings for the co-worker as trainer project. *Journal of Head Trauma Rehabilitation, 11*(1), 75-78.

Duncan, P. W. (1990). Physical therapy assessment. In M. Rosenthal, E. F. Griffith, M. F. Bond, & J. D. Miller (Eds.), Rehabilitation of the adult and child with traumatic brain injury (2nd ed., pp. 264-283). Philadelphia: F. A. Davis.

Fraser, R. T. (1991). Vocational evaluation. *Journal of Head Trauma Rehabilitation, 3*, 46-58.

Fraser, R., & Baarslag-Benson R. (1994). Cross disciplinary collaboration in the removal of work barriers after traumatic brain injury. *Topics in Language Disorders, 1*, 55-67.

Fraser, R. T., McMahon B. T., & Wehman P. (1991). *Traumatic brain injury vocational rehabilitation: Choice of a placement model.* Winter Park, FL: St. Lucie Press.

Golden, C. J., Hammeke, T., & Purisch, A. (1980). *The Luria-Nebraska neuropsychological battery: Manual.* (Rev ed.). Los Angeles: Western Psychological Services.

Gordon, L. (1981). *The Gordon occupational checklist II.* San Antonio: The Psychological Corp.

Institute for Personality and Ability Testing. (1991). *Sixteen personality factor questionnaire.* Champaign, IL: Author.

Job Accommodation Network. (1995, January). Morgantown, WV: West Virginia University.

McCarron, I., & Dial, J. (1976). *McCarron-Dial work evaluation system evaluation of the mentally disabled — A systematic approach.* Dallas: Common Market Press.

McMahon, B. T. (1986). Vocational programs and approaches that work. In B. G. Burns, T. Kay, & B. Pieper (Eds.), *A survey of the vocational service system as it relates to head injury survivors and their vocational needs.* Albany, NY: New York State Head Injury Association.

Millon, T. (1994). *Millon clinical multiaxial inventory III*. Minneapolis: National Computer Systems.

Nadolsky, J. (1985). Vocational evaluation: An experimental trend in assessment. In C. Smith & R. Fry (Eds.), *National forum on issues in vocational assessment: The issues papers*. Menomenee, WI: University of Wisconsin-Stout, Stout Vocational Rehabilitation Institute, Materials Development Center.

OASYS. (1993). Bellevue, WA: Vertec.

Reitan, R. M., & Wolfson, D. (1985). *The Halstead-Reitan neuropsychological test battery*. Tucson: Neuropsychological Press.

Roessler, R. T. (1988). *Worker performance assessment*. Little Rock: University of Arkansas. Arkansas Research and Training Center in Vocational Rehabilitation.

Teasdale, G., & Jennett, B. (1974). Assessment of coma and impaired consciousness: A practical scale. *Lancet, 2,* 81.

Thomas, D. (1990). *Vocational evaluation and traumatic brain injury*. Menomonee, WI: University of Wisconsin-Stout, Stout Vocational Rehabilitation Institute, Materials Development Center.

Uomoto, J. (1991). *The use of the neuropsychological evaluation in vocational planning*. Winter Park, FL: St. Lucie Press.

U.S. Office of Personnel Management. (1982). *Federal personnel manual*. Washington, DC: U.S. Government Printing Office.

U.S. Department of Labor. (1993). *Individual vocational rehabilitation programs: Transition of persons with disability into employment*. Washington, DC: U.S. Department of Labor, Employment Standards Administration, Wage and Hour Division.

Vocational Evaluation and Work Adjustment Association. (1975). *Vocational evaluation project final report*. Menomonee, WI: University of Wisconsin-Stout, Stout Vocational Rehabilitation Institute, Materials Development Center.

Warren, G. (1991). *Assistive technology in traumatic brain injury*. Winter Park, FL: St. Lucie Press.

Wechsler, D. (1981). *Manual for the Wechsler adult intelligence scale-revised (WAIS-R)*. San Antonio: The Psychological Corp.

Weed, R. O., & Field, E. S. (1990). *Rehabilitation consultants' handbook*. Athens, GA: Elliot & Fitzpatrick.

9

Vocational Rehabilitation for Patients with Schizophrenia

H. Richard Lamb, MD, and Cecile Mackota

Dr. Lamb is Professor of Psychiatry, University of Southern California School of Medicine, Los Angeles, CA. Ms. Mackota is the former Director of Vocational Rehabilitation, San Mateo County (California) Mental Health Services, San Mateo, CA.

KEY POINTS

- For patients with schizophrenia, the use of vocational rehabilitation services in conjunction with appropriate ongoing psychiatric treatment considerably increases the efficacy of both treatment approaches.

- Vocational rehabilitation with persons with schizophrenia can be extremely effective; it contributes to their mental health by increasing their feelings of self-esteem, and it often leads to their achieving a greater degree of independence through employment.

- Work therapy is directed to the healthy part of the person. The aim is to maximize strengths and not focus on psychopathology.

- A day treatment center should not be used as an ongoing, life-long resource for patients with schizophrenia. Combining work therapy and social therapy in a mix tailored to the needs of each individual is more appropriate and does not foster undue dependency and regression.

- Mental health professionals should guard against their tendency to view nonprofessional work as demeaning or monotonous. They should recognize that their patients' values may differ from their own; their patients may achieve a great sense of mastery and self-worth by succeeding in whatever job is within their capabilities.

INTRODUCTION

Vocational rehabilitation for patients with schizophrenia can bring a great deal of meaning to their lives. Referral of a patient by a psychiatrist to a rehabilitation counselor may lead to successful placement and contribute to the patient's well-being. This chapter provides a practical guide to the world of vocational rehabilitation and describes the role of the vocational rehabilitation counselor and the collaborative relationship between psychiatrist and counselor.

FURTHERING VOCATIONAL REHABILITATION

If work therapy is to be used to its fullest advantage, professionals need to guard against the tendency to view nonprofessional work in terms of their own subjective reaction to it. Concentrating on the aspects of work they themselves find dull, monotonous, even degrading, they often do not see that others may achieve a great sense of mastery and self-worth by success in whatever job is within their capabilities. To a large extent, lower-level or entry-level jobs and sheltered work activities may not be considered worthwhile; professionals often are preoccupied with the "monotony" of routine work and the nonintellectual nature of unprofessional work. As a result, the benefits that derive simply from working—the feeling of being productive, the sense of being needed, the social outlet (in terms of one's relationship with co-workers)—may be largely neglected.

Upwards-striving, high-achieving professionals must recognize that their patients' values may differ from their own and that their patients do not necessarily consider tasks requiring less cognitive skills demeaning. Doing any job well is generally highly regarded in circles other than those of many professionals.

For example, a young man recently discharged from a state hospital was able to leave a sheltered workshop after only 3 months and get a job as a dishwasher in a large, busy cafeteria. Understandably proud, he came to report this to his aftercare group. The response of the group leader was, "Isn't that great! That will help you to get a better job later." Insensitive to the patient's satisfaction, the professional, in a single sentence, destroyed his patient's joy by implicitly downgrading the achievement.

SOME CONCEPTIONS AND MISCONCEPTIONS

We believe that, to the extent possible, a day treatment center should not be used as an ongoing, lifelong resource for patients with schizophrenia. The alternative, which is much more appropriate and does not foster regression and undue dependency, is one that combines work therapy and social therapy in a mix tailored to the needs of each person. Before we can use work therapeutically, however, we must wade through a number of misconceptions.

Relationship Between Work and Recovery:

There is not, as many have supposed, a clear relationship between work capacity and degree of emotional recovery; that is, the ability to obtain a job and perform it does not require a certain degree of wellness. Some of the sickest and most disturbed people are able to work, some marginally and some with a high degree of competence. Also, it is often assumed that people have to be socialized before they are able to go to work, that they have to achieve a high enough level of social skills to get along with other people on some basis of reciprocity. Experienced clinicians know, however, that this is not necessarily the case. Some patients can act appropriately within a structured work situation when cues are available to guide them but may be immobilized and confused by the lack of structure in a social situation. Others may achieve a high level of social skills but still be unable or unwilling to work.

Relationship Between Work and Social Skills:

Work is seen by many patients as an activity that does not require them to exercise social skills. That makes it more comfortable than other activities. For instance, one patient said, "On my job I don't have to be me." What she meant was that while she was working, the nature of her job defined her; she was a "cashier," and all her social anxieties could be put aside while she concentrated on the tasks of a cashier. She understood clearly what she had to do and felt competent to carry out the specific activities connected with the job. By contrast, she was lost in social situations where she saw herself as having to chart her own course and meet standards that seemed to her frighteningly amorphous.

A related and important point is that sometimes, for the person with schizophrenia, stressing socialization is contraindicated. For example, a withdrawn young man had persistent difficulty in relating to others in social situations. He could, however, work effectively as an electronic assembler because his interaction with other workers was minimal and could be limited to job matters. In the course of therapy, the patient was encouraged to develop social skills and to try them out on the job. Within a short period, he had quit his job and required hospitalization. After some time, he was able to express the deep fears socialization had aroused in him because he could not determine what degree of socializing was appropriate to the various situations in which he found himself. He felt he had completely lost control and became so upset that he had to flee from the situation. The expectation that persons with schizophrenia will learn to socialize is not always realistic; many have demonstrated they can function much better when not asked to develop and use social skills.

Frequently, having gained a degree of self-confidence from being successful on a job, persons with schizophrenia can gradually begin to devote their energies to performing better in social situations. For this reason, some are placed very early in a work situation rather than in a day treatment center or any other treatment requiring free social interaction with others. Such placement allows them to work on their interpersonal interactions gradually while engaged in a structured work task.

The Role of Sheltered Employment:

Many persons with disabilities, for a variety of reasons, cannot be rehabilitated into regular competitive employment. They lack either the capacity or the will to meet the rigorous demands of most employers. For this group, sheltered workshops or other sheltered work arrangements are needed. An example of the latter would be an arrangement with a private employer in which a job in a factory or a store is performed by a vocational rehabilitation patient accompanied by a counselor, who may at first help the patient perform the work. Sometimes two patients may share one job, one in the morning and one in the afternoon. Having a reason to get up in the morning, having a place to go where one can be useful and productive, earning money, having friends, and feeling accepted can be a tremendously important factor in the life of a person for whom the alternative is sitting in a board and care home watching television.

Nor can we assume that all persons with schizophrenia will remain in need of ongoing sheltered employment. Some for whom we would predict little improvement will surprise us and ultimately go on to competitive employment. There should be no limit on how long persons with schizophrenia can remain in a sheltered employment setting and no pressure on them to leave. When they are ready to move on, they find ways to let us know.

The Rationale for Work Therapy:

Work therapy must have a well thought-out rationale. Using work only to provide a daytime activity accomplishes little in the way of rehabilitation. How serious and important therapists feel the work task is, and how they communicate their attitudes, consciously or unconsciously, to their patients has a profound impact on the effectiveness of work therapy. To begin with, professionals must maintain the same attitude whether or not the work involves competitive employment. If the tasks patients are doing are made to seem of little consequence, then they cannot see either the tasks or themselves as being valuable. Professionals communicate in verbal or non-verbal ways their reaction to low-level, low-pay jobs, and they need to guard against such disclosures in reacting to their patients' work activities. For most of their patients, work has been an important, integral part of their lives, and in our culture, our work still remains one of the major means by which we take our place in the mainstream of life.

CONCEPTS UNDERLYING WORK THERAPY

Work therapy is directed to the healthy part of the person. The aim is to maximize strengths and not focus on psychopathology. Work therapy focuses on reality factors rather than on intrapsychic phenomena and on changing behavior rather than on changing basic character structure. Work therapy can make the difference between a life of regression, dependency, and depression on the one hand and a life with considerable gratification and a sense of mastery on the other.

An example will illustrate some of these points. A workshop patient is sitting at her work station hallucinating and not working. The trained foreman says to the patient, "Stop talking back to the voices and get back to work." The foreman is talking to the well part of the ego. He is applying the concept of high but realistic expectations by conveying to the worker with schizophrenia that she is capable of being productive and is expected to strive to realize her potential. He is emphasizing to the patient her identity as a worker rather than as a patient. He is using a direct approach that reaches the patient. He is helping the patient achieve control. Further, he is indicating to the patient that he cares about her instead of simply allowing her to sit there preoccupied with her psychotic symptomatology.

Whether we are talking about a sheltered work setting or some other work setting such as an entry-level job, we must emphasize that in work therapy, we are using sophisticated techniques even though at first they may appear simple. Work therapy is often seen as nonintellectual by therapists unfamiliar with it; and, because it does not involve an intellectual discussion of psychodynamics, a superficial look at this type of therapy may confirm that opinion. However, important concepts underlie work therapy.

Mastery:

Mastery is one concept of work therapy. Patients' feelings of accomplishment and their knowledge that they have been able to perform a task whose value is proved to them (because they have been paid money for it and because the work has resulted in a useful product) gives them a sense of mastery, a feeling that they are not powerless and helpless in the world. The dependent patient role can be discarded gradually as the identity of "worker" is assumed. Contrary to what is thought in many circles, patients *must* receive vocational counseling throughout this process to give substance to what they are doing and to evaluate and consolidate their gains or losses. The counselor's role is discussed in greater detail later in this chapter.

Expectations:

Also involved is the concept of high but realistic expectations. This concept does not require that every person with schizophrenia achieve competitive employment. Rather, for each person, the expectation is that he or she perform at his or her highest level of capacity. For example, in a sheltered workshop, if the highest possible level for a particular patient is 50% of what workers in industry would be able to achieve, then 50% is a high expectation for this particular person. But if he or she is able to achieve 50%, we should not be satisfied — or let the patient be satisfied — with 25%. Patients with schizophrenia respond to these expectations in a positive way in terms of both achievement and self-esteem, and the professionals working with them need to communicate clearly what the expectations are. An attitude of high but realistic expectations tells patients in a meaningful way that others see them as more competent than they themselves supposed and that they are capable of achieving at a higher level.

The same principle of high but realistic expectations should be applied to the person with schizophrenia's behavior in any type of training or work activity. If we give the patient the clear, consistent message that we expect a certain kind of performance and will not accept craziness, apathy, or a rationalization such as, "I can't do that, I'm handicapped," then we are likely to get a better level of performance and a healthier response. It is important that this attitude be enunciated as well as implied by our actions.

VOCATIONAL REHABILITATION COUNSELING

The attitude among some professionals that vocational rehabilitation counselors should play a relatively unimportant part, or no part at all, in the treatment of patients with schizophrenia is fairly common. The basis for this viewpoint is the fact that a substantial percentage of these patients will not enter the competitive labor market. However, the intrinsic value of work therapy makes quality rehabilitation counseling a necessity whether or not the goal is regular employment. Certainly, how much counseling, what kind, and when it is used will depend on the needs of the individual patient. This would be true in working with any patient category. But work therapy attempted without the particular skills of a rehabilitation counselor has greatly diminished potential.

In what ways can the counselor work more effectively in this area than other helping professionals? It is true that the function of a counselor often seems indistinguishable from that of a psychotherapist. The important difference, however, lies in the counselor's orientation to the occupational aspects of life, his or her special knowledge in the field, and a focus on accomplishing behavior change with regard to work. Purposely setting aside other areas of the person's life, the counselor focuses on vocational planning and vocational activities. The counselor's conviction is, however, that successes in these areas enhance other therapy and facilitate change in other facets of the person's life.

Appropriate Patients for Referral:

Psychiatrists often ask what kind of patient should be referred for vocational rehabilitation services. Counselors are apt to reply that anyone who expresses any interest at all and who can get to a facility should at least have the opportunity to be considered for such services. Assessment by a professional vocational rehabilitation counselor may bring different results than the referring psychiatrist might have expected. Sometimes, patients who appeared to the psychiatrist to be questionable referrals seem highly appropriate in the judgment of the counselor, and vice versa. Counselors and therapists see patients with schizophrenia from different perspectives.

Patients also may present themselves very differently to the counselor. When patients with schizophrenia see a psychiatrist in a psychiatric setting, they usually will conform to the role expectations of the environment and behave like patients, so their employment potential may not be evident. On the other hand, they may express a desire to work to their psychiatrists because they want their psychiatrists to perceive them as persons who want to work, although in actuality they may be extremely fearful of work and not ready to consider it. In their discussion about work with the vocational counselor, patients themselves may see these realities, or they become plain to the counselor.

Timing of Referral:

Although referral of patients with schizophrenia should be made as early as possible, it should not be made at an unpropitious time. Patients can derive little benefit from vocational rehabilitation if their energies are totally involved with a divorce, a separation, the loss of a loved one, or a major change in lifestyle. The psychiatrist, however, should be sensitive to the very beginnings of recovery from crisis and help patients become involved in work activity before they settle into a life pattern of apathy and inactivity.

The vocational rehabilitation counselor is involved with patients with schizophrenia throughout the rehabilitation process. In their early contacts, counselors probably need to take a more active, authoritative role than they would normally assume with their other patients. It may be some time before persons with severe disabilities can take positive action on their own — and an even longer time before they allow themselves to believe that there is any hope that they can operate effectively. A less active approach should, of course, be taken as soon as patients are able to take on self-direction.

Initial Steps:

Following referral, counselors and patients will be assessing each other and working together to determine immediate plans. Frequently for patients with schizophrenia, the sheltered workshop is a good beginning. At this point, the counselors' concern will be that the patients be clear about what they hope to accomplish in the workshop. Counselors will have reviewed the patients' employment history and will have made some judgments about employment potential as well as which behaviors would have to be adjusted before successful and satisfying employment could be reached. With these judgments in mind, counselors can help patients identify problems to be dealt with in the workshop. Counselors must be cautious in this determination and plan for simple goals that patients will have no trouble reaching.

Continued Monitoring:

During the time the patients are in the workshop, regular meetings with the counselors should be scheduled so that progress can be assessed and new goals can be set or expectations reduced. Counselors should be open with patients with schizophrenia because they will likely respond with a similar openness and deal with real issues. To illustrate, a workshop patient on a medication that produces tremulousness if taken alone consistently came to the workshop without taking his antiparkinsonism medication. He would say he had forgotten and would have to go home to take it, thus losing several hours of work time. The counselor felt free to say, "Several times in the past 2 weeks you have missed hours of work because you had to return home for your medication. I think you are trying to tell us you don't want to be here." With the situation clearly spelled out and in the open, the patient could then discuss his real concern—not really wanting to work, feeling resentful because he felt his wife and therapist were forcing him to come, and fearing that eventually he would have to face a job that was beyond his capabilities.

Persons with schizophrenia sometimes can tolerate only limited amounts of closeness, and contacts may be short and limited to the workshop floor. For instance, one patient, who has now been employed for 4 years, was at first unable to tolerate as brief a period as 10 minutes in the counselor's office. She would sit on the edge of the chair and protest continually that she wasn't worth the counselor's taking any time with her. Because of her evident discomfort, the patient was seen only during work, for a short conversation or greeting. It was not until she came to the counselor's office and requested an appointment that regular interviews were set up. Even then, they were never more than 15–20 minutes long. Eventually she was able to stay in the counselor's office without discomfort.

A rather common outcome of the patient-counselor relationship in work with patients with schizophrenia is the discovery that a person who has the intellectual capacity or aptitude for certain careers has neither the emotional strength nor the personality characteristics to succeed in those fields. An in-depth knowledge of occupational requirements is necessary to reach and act on this conclusion. Counselors are aware of the ingredients that make up the work environment of the various occupations and the essential personality traits required. Conversely, knowledge of the patient will suggest to the counselor those occupational fields that will be compatible with his or her personality.

Sometimes this knowledge is used to reinforce the appropriateness of the patient's current job, and psychotherapy can then focus on the real problems without resorting to "geographic therapy" (change of jobs). An excellent example of such reinforcement is a 42-year-old engineer who has schizophrenia and who had been in therapy since the age of 15. He had been able to achieve an excellent employment history despite the severity of his illness. He was employed on an experimental electronics project, usually working alone in a situation that was low key and relatively unpressured. He was referred for vocational counseling and testing to find another kind of work he could perform because he believed a recent exacerbation of his illness was caused by his job. Following counseling and a battery of vocational interest and aptitude tests, it was clear that the job in which he was engaged was uniquely suited to him. He and his psychiatrist then were able to explore other areas in his life and pinpoint why he was particularly troubled at that time.

For many patients with schizophrenia who express a desire to work, it will become clear that there is little or no possibility that work outside a sheltered setting can be considered. Here, the counselor's role will be to alleviate anxiety about "not progressing" and give support to the patient in what he or she is doing in the sheltered work setting. In this instance, the counselor's attention to the details of a continuing evaluation reassures the patient of the value of his or her work activity. Furthermore, in this way, the door is left open for future spontaneous change and improvement that can occur even in very regressed patients.

It is noteworthy that some persons with schizophrenia believe that going to work is their only way "back into society." Working is so equated with normalcy in our society that it becomes a major criterion of "wellness." For this reason, vocational rehabilitation adds another important dimension to the treatment of patients with schizophrenia.

INTERACTION BETWEEN VOCATIONAL REHABILITATION COUNSELORS AND PSYCHIATRISTS

Wise psychiatrists are aware that they cannot be expected to have expertise in all areas, so most comfortably refer patients to specialists in other fields. Vocational counselors are outside of their own role in attempting psychotherapy, and they do a disservice to their patients if they attempt it. So it is with most psychiatrists who attempt vocational counseling and career selection; they are not serving their patients as well as they might by a judicious referral to a person with vocational rehabilitation skills.

In referring a patient for vocational rehabilitation services, some psychiatrists specify a particular activity: "Needs sheltered workshop," for example, or, "Place in training to be a landscape gardener's assistant." However, better results can be obtained if the psychiatrist simply refers the person for a vocational evaluation and whatever services subsequently appear indicated. In this way, the psychiatrist allows the counselor and the patient to work out vocational plans unhindered. The patient who arrives unannounced at the vocational services center, lunch in hand, and prepared to enter a sheltered workshop setting "because the doctor sent me," is rarely able to consider other plans without a great deal of difficulty. Patients may look almost totally different than they appeared to the psychiatrist, and a sheltered work setting may not turn out to be the best plan.

Somewhat along the same lines is the psychiatrist's encouragement of a particular vocational aspiration for the sake of supporting any positive activity on the part of the patient. Frequently, and understandably, the psychiatrist sees an interest in a vocation as a healthy sign, takes that interest at face value, and fosters it with no real discrimination. For instance, a person may say he wants to be an electronics technician, and the psychiatrist agrees that the idea is a good one. This endorsement from the psychiatrist without any determination of the patient's fine finger dexterity, mathematical ability, patience with minute detail, or even possible color blindness, usually results in the patient's adamantly pursuing that career selection no matter how inappropriate. Rather, the psychiatrist could have responded, "I'm glad to see that you are thinking along the lines of considering employment. Why don't you discuss this with your vocational counselor? She might also have some other ideas you would want to consider." In this way, the door would have been left open for other options. The rehabilitation counselor in consultation with the psychiatrist can be of great service by suggesting to the psychiatrist this approach at the onset of the partnership.

This is particularly appropriate when patient and psychiatrist have unrealistic ideas of the capabilities and readiness of the patient. A good example of this is a referral of a 47-year-old housewife with the notation, "Needs a job right away to get her out of the house." This patient had a 20-year history of multiple hospitalizations for schizophrenia and had not worked since she was 21. She had no work skills, appeared withdrawn and fearful, and had no idea of the kind of work she would like to do. She came prepared to have the counselor produce some magic results, and when these were not forthcoming, she gave up and did not keep further appointments.

CONCLUSION

Work therapy with patients with schizophrenia can be an extremely effective activity that not only helps them remain in the community but also makes their lives more meaningful. Vocational rehabilitation contributes to the mental health of patients with schizophrenia by increasing their feelings of self-esteem and mastery over their lives, and it often leads to their achieving a greater degree of independence through employment. The use of vocational rehabilitation services in conjunction with appropriate ongoing psychiatric therapy considerably increases the efficacy of both treatment approaches.

FOR FURTHER READING

Bachrach, L. L. (1992). Psychosocial rehabilitation and psychiatry in the care of long-term patients. *American Journal of Psychiatry, 149*, 1455-1463.

Dincin, J. (Ed.). (1995). A pragmatic approach to psychiatric rehabilitation: Lessons from Chicago's thresholds program. *New Directions for Mental Health Services, 68.*

Lamb, H. R. (1994). A century and a half of psychiatric rehabilitation in the United States. *Hospital and Community Psychiatry, 45*, 1015-1020.

Liberman, R. P. (Ed.). (1992). Effective psychiatric rehabilitation. *New Directions for Mental Health Services, 53.*

10

Cultural Diversity and Its Impact on Career Counseling

Jay W. Rojewski, PhD

Dr. Rojewski is Associate Professor, Department of Occupational Studies, The University of Georgia, Athens, GA.

KEY POINTS

- Because of demographic changes in the United States, rehabilitation counselors are beginning to encounter more ethnic minority clients. Demographic projections indicate that within 20 years, minorities will become a numerical majority of the U.S. population.

- This growth in the ethnic minority population may lead to unprecedented employment opportunities for members of minority groups who are adequately prepared to take advantage of them; however, racism, job discrimination, and other obstacles will continue to present challenges to minorities in finding and maintaining employment.

- Rehabilitation and career counselors must closely examine the growing and changing problems and needs of job seekers of minority backgrounds and cultivate

an awareness of how diverse cultural beliefs and values influence the career planning and preparation process.

- Counselors also must discern the extent to which their clients identify and practice the culture of their ancestors. Three important factors to consider are: level of acculturation, racial identity, and the presence of risk factors.

- The values, beliefs, and world views of different cultures should influence the way rehabilitation services are provided. This chapter examines major characteristics, values, and career-related problems attributed to the four cultural/ethnic minority groups most frequently encountered by rehabilitation professionals: African Americans, Hispanics, Asians, and Native Americans.

INTRODUCTION

The increase in the number of new refugees and immigrants in the United States, the changing nature of our labor market conditions, and a heightened appreciation of the important role that culture plays in career choice and the career counseling process (Helms & Piper, 1994; Wright, 1988) virtually demand that rehabilitation professionals cultivate an awareness and understanding of how diverse cultural beliefs and values influence the career planning and preparation process. However, the most immediate reason for this emphasis is that rehabilitation counselors are beginning to encounter more minority clients, who reflect the constantly changing demographic landscape of American society (Atkins, 1992; Swanson, 1993).

Demographic projections indicate that the percentage of persons representing all minority groups (nonwhite) in the workforce will increase from approximately 17% in the late 1980s to more than 25% by the year 2000 (Kutscher, 1990). Within 20 years, racial and ethnic minorities will become a numerical majority, and white Americans will constitute slightly less than half the U.S. population (Sue, Arredondo, & McDavis, 1992). An issue of direct concern to rehabilitation counselors is the speculation that a large percentage of this emerging ethnic minority population will experience disabilities (Wright, 1988).

Hawks and Muha (1991) believe that demographic changes may lead to unprecedented employment opportunities in our society for members of minority groups who are adequately prepared to take advantage of them. Unfortunately, adolescents from minority groups are often the least prepared for jobs demanding high levels of technologic skill. This lack of preparation of adolescents, particularly those who are African American or Hispanic, can be evidenced partly in the disproportionately higher high-school drop-out rates for these groups as compared with their white counterparts (Kutscher, 1990). Even with adequate preparation, ethnic and cultural minorities with disabilities encounter myriad obstacles and barriers in finding and maintaining employment, including occupational stereotyping, racism, and discrimination as a result of the combination of minority group status *and* the presence of a physical or mental impairment. Given these formidable challenges, it quickly becomes apparent that rehabilitation personnel must closely examine current practices in relation to the growing and changing problems and needs experienced by culturally diverse job seekers.

Although it is important to make a conscious decision to understand and serve minority groups, commitment alone is not enough. The literature contains numerous articles that point to the widespread ineffectiveness of traditional counseling approaches and techniques when applied to racial and ethnic minority populations (Anderson, Wang, & Houser, 1993; Leung & Sakata, 1988; Smith, 1980; Tinsley, 1994; Wright, 1988).

CHARACTERISTICS AND WORLD VIEWS OF CULTURALLY DIVERSE POPULATIONS

This section briefly highlights major characteristics, values, and career-related problems attributed to four cultural/ethnic minority groups most often encountered by rehabilitation practitioners — African Americans, Hispanics, Asians, and Native Americans. This general overview is not intended to be a complete cultural description of these four groups; descriptions are not presented to stereotype or ignore within-group differences but to illustrate common barriers to career choice and employment typically encountered by these minority groups. Tinsley (1994, p. 115) explains:

> It seems obvious that a somewhat different configuration of factors influences the career development of persons of different cultural and racial heritage. Despite their individuality, people from the same culture share common experiences that

help to shape their attitudes, values, expectations, and aspirations. Individuals from different cultural backgrounds can be expected to differ in the expectations, aspirations, and values they bring to the career development process. As a result, they encounter different problems and barriers which they must resolve, and they differ in their attitudes about the career development process.

"Within any given group, there may be additional differences important to understanding individual and family attitudes and perceptions" (Leung & Sakata, 1988, p. 18). One should keep this caveat in mind while confronting various characteristics and problems lest one subordinate the uniquely human characteristics and individual needs of each client to stereotypes of the culture to which he or she belongs (Fouad, 1993; Smart & Smart, 1990).

African Americans:

African Americans are the largest and most researched ethnic minority group in the United States (Bowman, 1993). Detailed descriptions of the cultural and vocational characteristics of African Americans abound in the literature. In general, the literature supports the existence of an authentic "Black self" and tends to stress the existence of a collective (group-centered and interdependent) and affective (sensitive to interpersonal matters) orientation in African-American culture (Brown, 1990; Herbert & Cheatham, 1988). Parham and Austin (1994, p. 146) summarized these cultural characteristics:

> African Americans are more prone to be collective and group-oriented vs. individual/self-oriented; supportive and interdependent vs. competitive; affective/feelings-oriented vs. rational/cognitively oriented; relationship/person-to-person-oriented vs. task/things (commodities)-oriented; orally expressive vs. written; and developing a sense of harmony with the universe vs. control and domination.

African-American culture attaches less stigma to disability than do many other cultures. Feelings of protection and acceptance are typical responses of African Americans toward persons with disabilities (Marion, 1980). Key cultural values, which include reliance on extended family networks for support and assistance, open and free expression of emotion, general orientations toward interpersonal situations rather than the world of objects, and strong religious beliefs, contribute to a more accepting and mutually supportive approach to persons with disabilities and also lessen the negative stigma attached to the presence of a disability (Turner, 1987). In addition, prejudice and other societal barriers have created a situation in which survival for African Americans requires the ability to adapt (Jenkins & Amos, 1983). "Consequently, the birth of a disabled or high-risk child happens into a cultural system that has been molded to accommodate crisis" (Turner, 1987, p. 14). These cultural attributes and experiences often provide persons with disabilities and their families the physical and emotional support needed to cope adequately with problems associated with disabilities. However, these same attributes may instill a general mistrust and reluctance to solicit the help of persons or agencies outside one's extended family (let alone culture).

Studies of African Americans typically have reported slower rates of career development for this group as compared with the majority population (Luzzo, 1992). The vocational literature often portrays African Americans as vocationally handicapped, attitudinally negative toward work, and generally less satisfied with their careers (Smith, 1980). A number of reasons for these problems have been suggested, including a lack of positive work-related experiences, a lack of visible role models in nontraditional fields, restricted access to career and employment information, and stereotypes about the types of jobs that African Americans traditionally hold (e.g., employment in the helping professions or in areas that involve working with people) (Dunn & Veltman, 1989; Herbert & Cheatham, 1988). It is important to examine these issues because African-

American consumers in rehabilitation programs tend to receive fewer and less costly services and are less successful in obtaining employment than white Americans (Atkins & Wright, 1980).

Hispanic Americans:.

Hispanic Americans represent one of the largest, yet least acculturated, ethnic groups in this country. Limited acculturation is the result of traditional values passed from one generation to the next, as well as a strong commitment of many Hispanic Americans to maintain a common language. The Hispanic population represents a number of distinct, separate subgroups, including Mexican Americans, Puerto Ricans, and persons who trace their origins to Central or South America. Hispanic Americans also may be of any race, which means the within-group diversity of this population is pronounced and must be considered in the rehabilitation process.

Smart and Smart (1990) warned against the tendency to "lump" various Hispanic subcultures together because each subgroup adheres to different beliefs, values, and customs. Even so, available evidence suggests that, as a group, Hispanic Americans experience higher levels of poverty, undereducation, unemployment, mobility, poor health, and disability than the majority population.

A feature that distinguishes Hispanic culture from the majority culture is a strong family tradition. Hispanic families tend to be hierarchical in nature, often include an extended social network, and are strongly male dominated (Correa, 1987). The influence of women is usually more subtle but cannot be discounted, particularly because Hispanic men often defer important family decisions to women (deMateo-Smith, 1987). The hierarchical nature of Hispanic culture is further reinforced through the practice of giving older siblings the responsibility of looking after younger siblings (Correa, 1987; Mardiros, 1989). Hispanic mothers tend to be overprotective of their children and keep them dependent longer than white children. This practice usually is intensified and extended for a child with a disability often creating dependency, immaturity, and isolation. As a result, rehabilitation counselors may find it difficult to develop self-sufficiency and independence skills in their Hispanic clients.

A strong family unit is a great source of pride and respect for most Hispanic Americans. Indeed, individual accomplishments and actions are viewed as a direct reflection on the entire family. However, this sense of family pride may lead to attempts at hiding or sheltering children with disabilities from society, lest the family be viewed as less than ideal or less worthy of the respect of others. Although most Hispanic families eventually accept and support a family member with a disability, the presence of such a member often is accompanied by a deep sense of shame and guilt (Correa, 1987; Mardiros, 1989). Interestingly, the tendency to hide a child with a disability from others may be greater for families of higher socioeconomic status (deMateo-Smith, 1987).

A second factor is a combination of spiritual and folk beliefs about the cause of disabilities. Although a majority of Hispanic people profess a strong commitment to Roman Catholicism, many also adhere to spiritual folk beliefs. Together, these beliefs result in a number of explanations regarding the presence of a disability, including divine intervention (i.e., God's will), punishment for the past sins of parents or ancestors, or the presence of evil spirits. Regardless of the specific cause attributed to the disability, Hispanic parents often feel personally responsible for their child's disability (Garza, 1986; Mardiros, 1989).

To date, the literature identifies a number of common problems that affect the career development and vocational rehabilitation efforts of Hispanic clients with disabilities, including the effects of social problems (e.g., poverty and racism), lack of technologic skills, low placement expectations, job placement discrimination, problems with standardized tests, and, in some cases, limited proficiency in the English language (Smart & Smart, 1993). Because of these problems, Hispanic Americans are less likely to trust systems established and maintained by the dominant culture or to cooperate with service providers in these systems, including vocational rehabilitation personnel. For a comprehensive, practical examination of vocational evaluation of Hispanic clients, see Chapter 11.

Asian Americans:

Asian Americans represent a rapidly growing minority group in the United States and often have been referred to as a "model" minority, capable of success and achievement within the majority culture. However, this belief is misleading and can interfere seriously with achieving goals set forth in the rehabilitation process. Asian Americans are not a homogeneous group; they represent at least thirty-two distinct ethnic or cultural groups, possessing unique and varied characteristics, problems, and cultural backgrounds predicated on unique languages, customs, and traditions. Although tremendous diversity exists in this minority group, certain common characteristics may be useful in understanding any particular subgroup.

A prevalent attribute of Asian-American culture is the focus on hierarchical interpersonal relationships with strong respect and loyalty to family and authority. In many Asian-American homes, the needs of the family and family honor are placed ahead of personal interests and concerns. Humility and modesty in social interactions also are valued highly. Asian Americans value a collective rather than individual orientation, which is reflected in their reliance on family members for support and comfort when important decisions are made. Issues of honor and avoiding a "loss of face" also are very important. In response to these values, Asian Americans have developed elaborate, subtle, and complex forms of interpersonal communication, including nonverbal cues (Leong, 1991, 1993).

Despite the recent growth of Asian-American culture, relatively limited information is available about the career development of this group. One noteworthy investigation has revealed that Asian Americans score lower in affective career maturity and are more likely to display a dependent career decision-making style as compared with their white peers (Leong, 1991; Luzzo, 1992). (*Career maturity* can be defined as one's feelings, subjective reactions, and dispositions toward making a career choice as well as toward entering the workforce.) Another interesting finding is that the prestige level of potential careers is an unusually important variable in the career choice of many Asian Americans. Leung (1993, p. 192) found that Asian Americans "may weigh prestige exceedingly highly in making a career-related decision, ignoring other factors, such as personal interests and aptitudes."

The presence of a disability is viewed with considerable stigma in Asian-American culture and may be a source of overwhelming family shame and embarrassment. Asian-American parents tend to be traumatized more than other parents by the birth of a child with a disability and remain in denial longer. The tremendous stigma that Asian Americans attach to a disability may result, in part, from the causes they attribute to it. One common explanation of a disability is that the condition represents punishment for past sins committed by parents or other family members. Some Asian Americans, particularly those with a low level of acculturation, may believe that a person with a disability is possessed by an evil spirit or demon. Another explanation suggests that a disability is the result of an imbalance in the person's mind-body relationship. It is evident from these explanations that the presence of a disability presumes some type of imbalance or problem. This, in turn, places the honor of the family in question; not surprisingly, the loss of honor or respect is something Asian-American families wish to avoid at all costs (Leung, 1987; Morrow, 1987).

Knowledge of Asian-American cultural values, beliefs, and career development has implications for rehabilitation practice. For example, many Asian Americans believe that life is unalterable and unpredictable. This world view results in a fatalistic resignation to external conditions and events over which there is little or no *perceived* control. The ability to endure and live with hardship is considered an important cultural virtue for Asian Americans. This world view reduces the likelihood that persons with disabilities will actively seek rehabilitative services. In addition, Asian Americans who receive services may be less active in their own rehabilitation (Leung, 1987).

Another important consideration centers on the issue of counseling approach and communication. "A common observation among counselors who have provided counseling to Asian Americans is the *difficulty of obtaining direct, spontaneous, and accurate feedback about the therapeutic process.* . . . Such direct forms of communication alienate many Asian Americans who consider it rude to provide direct negative communication" (Leong, 1993, p. 28) (emphasis added).

Native Americans:

Native-American culture in this country is extremely varied and has been influenced by repeated attempts over the past several hundred years to weaken or destroy tribal languages, customs, and beliefs. Despite tremendous diversity, generalized values seem to permeate all Native-American cultures (LaFromboise, 1988). For example, many Native Americans share a world view that presumes a holistic and harmonious relationship among and within persons, society, and nature. This perspective is supported and nurtured through extended family structures that emphasize interdependence, reciprocity, and mutual obligation. Work-related activities usually are group oriented rather than based on individual need or status attainment (Atkinson, Morten, & Sue, 1993; LoneWolf-Miller & Joe, 1993). Native-American cultures often promote generosity in sharing of self, resources, and possessions; honor past traditions; do not rigidly structure time (i.e., believe in "taking life as it comes"); and encourage respectful, discrete communication with minimal eye contact and an emphasis on listening (Clark & Kelly, 1992).

Native Americans often attribute psychological and physical illness or disability to human weakness and a lack of self-discipline in maintaining cultural values and community respect (LaFromboise, Trimble, & Mohatt, 1990). Thomason (1991) explained that breaking a taboo or ignoring a tradition can result in a state of disharmony which can be manifested in an individual as disability, disease, or distress. The strong social bonds of extended families and tribal ties influence the reaction of Native Americans to persons with disabilities. Individual problems are viewed as community (tribal) problems, resulting in less stigma attached to the disability and greater emphasis on providing support for the person with the disability (Atkinson et al., 1993). This may result in a view that vocational rehabilitation is a family-centered rather than a client-centered experience (Clark & Kelly, 1992).

Compared with other cultural groups, little is known about the career behavior of Native Americans. Two aspects of Native-American life—the existence of numerous negative stereotypes and disability rates that are higher than those found in the general population—undoubtedly influence the career choice and development of persons in this cultural group (Brown, 1990). On the whole, Native Americans experience limited career awareness and understanding. One explanation for this may be that Native Americans have so many environmental constraints that vocational choice and development may seem rather unimportant (Martin, 1991). Lower career awareness also may reflect the practice of many Native Americans to assign adult identities based on the relationships one has with the family, tribe, and friends rather than by a person's work roles. Undoubtedly, a lack of marketable job skills, poor health, low levels of education, and impoverished lifestyles are other obstacles to successful and satisfactory employment for many Native Americans (LoneWolf-Miller & Joe, 1993).

DETERMINING THE INFLUENCE OF CULTURE ON BEHAVIOR

A variety of factors contribute to the degree of influence that cultural beliefs and values have on determining a person's unique world view and, in turn, views toward disability, employment, and vocational rehabilitation. In addition to an awareness of clients' cultural backgrounds, rehabilitation counselors also must determine the extent to which their clients identify with and practice the culture of their ancestors. Three of the most important factors to consider when determining the influence of culture on behavior are the level of acculturation, racial identity, and the presence of risk factors.

Level of Acculturation:

Acculturation, which refers to the degree that cultural beliefs, values, and characteristics of a new or dominant culture have been acquired or adopted by a person from a minority group, can be a powerful determinant on the influence that culture has on behavior and attitudes, including career development. Persons with a high level of acculturation will exhibit cultural patterns similar to the same-age cohort of the dominant culture. Conversely, persons with low levels of acculturation will maintain traditional cultural values and customs (Atkinson et al., 1993).

Rehabilitation counselors should consider the influence of acculturation on their clients because it might have a profound effect on the way their clients perceive and respond to rehabilitation counseling, including preferences for counselors, perceptions of trustworthiness, vocational evaluation, job placement, and adherence to medical regimens (Smart & Smart, 1993). A person's level of acculturation may be influenced by a number of factors, including generational status, language preferences, occupational and educational status, and frequency of visits to one's original country (Comas-Diaz, 1993).

Racial/Ethnic Identity:

In recent years, counselors have begun to realize that the attitudes and behaviors of clients from minority backgrounds result, at least in part, from the way that clients identify with their own culture. Racial/ethnic identity is viewed as a developmental process that reflects a premise that all people, regardless of race, experience a stagewise development of racial consciousness (Helms, 1984). A person's racial identity can be determined by posing two basic questions: "How does a culturally diverse client view his or her own culture?" and "How does a culturally diverse client view the dominant host culture?" (Leong & Chou, 1994).

Racial identity includes five stages of development: (a) conformity/preencouter, (b) dissonance/encounter, (c) resistance/immersion, (d) internalization, and (e) integrative awareness (Atkinson et al., 1993; Cross, 1994; Evans & Herr, 1944).

1. In the *conformity/preencounter* stage, persons from minority groups state a preference for dominant cultural standards and values and may deny or devalue their own racial heritage. They often devalue their self-worth, see themselves as less desirable, and are likely to adopt stereotypes espoused by the dominant culture pertaining to personal characteristics and career options.

2. Movement to the *dissonance/encounter* stage often is precipitated by experiences that contradict a person's previous views of the dominant culture. Confusion, guilt, or anxiety may be experienced as a growing sense of cultural pride emerges and challenges self-definition and commitment to the dominant cultural group.

3. The *resistance/immersion* stage is characterized by a complete endorsement and idealization of one's own cultural affiliation while totally devaluing and rejecting the dominant culture. Information about one's history and culture becomes a source of pride; the beliefs and values of the dominant culture now tend to evoke feelings of distrust.

4. During the *internalization* stage, persons acquire an internally defined sense of group values and realize that not everything about the dominant culture is negative.

5. The final stage, *integrative awareness,* is defined by a sense of inner security and self-fulfillment. Interactions with other groups, even the cultural majority, are viewed as positive and beneficial.

The development of racial identity helps to explain the evolution of one's racial consciousness and its effects on counseling, career development, career choice patterns, and work-related satisfaction of minority clients (Cross, 1994; Helms, 1984; Helms & Piper, 1994; Parham & Austin, 1994). Knowledge about a client's stage of development may explain his or her preference for a counselor from the same culture, why particular career paths do not appeal to a client, or provide reasons for hostile or noncompliant behavior.

Risk Factors:

The career behavior of persons from minority backgrounds often is described from a deficiency or deficit perspective; that is, the world views and career behavior of cultural minority groups are compared with white middle-class values and behavior. Any differences found between the two groups are explained as inherent or unchangeable deficiencies of the minority culture (Sue et al., 1992).

Gottfredson (1986) offered an alternate explanation for understanding the career choice problems of cultural minority populations by asserting that *all* people experience some type of career-related problems based on the presence of certain risk factors. Potential risk factors are organized into three categories:

1. Factors used in comparison with the general

population (e.g., poor education, poverty, low self-esteem, and functional limitations)

2. Factors used in comparison within one's own social group (e.g., nontraditional interests and social isolation)

3. Factors involved in a person's family responsibilities (e.g., being a primary caregiver or economic provider)

Therefore, all groups (even white men) are at risk in some areas related to career behavior (the risks of white men are simply different). It is important to consider how these factors may influence the rehabilitation process, because minority groups may experience a higher-than-average probability of being at risk.

Comparisons with the General Population

Factors used to compare minority groups with the general population may hold the greatest likelihood of posing career-related problems. Many minority groups share several risk factors (Atkins, 1992). Perhaps the most prominent problem experienced by minority populations is social isolation due to discrimination, bias, or limited proficiency in the English language. The degree of isolation may be intensified further by the presence of a disability.

Data clearly indicate that African Americans, Hispanics, and Native Americans with disabilities are more likely to live in poverty or experience significant financial limitations as compared with white Americans. This relationship is even more pronounced for women (Smart & Smart, 1990). Persons from minority groups with disabilities often possess poor academic preparation and skills due to inferior educational opportunities (Brown, 1990). Moreover, they are more likely to drop out of school before earning a high school diploma (Asian-American adolescents are the exception). Even with educational opportunities, "the same educational benefits do not yield the same economic rewards" for members of minority groups (Smart & Smart, 1993, p. 173).

Low self-esteem often has been cited as a result of experiencing discrimination and negative stereotyping. Some aspects of self-esteem (e.g., self-efficacy and locus of control) differ by race and gender. However, Gottfredson (1986) warned that we cannot assume a person with a disability who is also a member of a particular racial or ethnic group will *automatically* experience a higher risk of low self-esteem.

Comparisons Within One's Own Social Group

Minority populations also may experience career-choice problems when compared with persons in the same social group. The combination of a disability and cultural/ethnic minority group status presents a double bias against many rehabilitation clients (Herbert & Cheatham, 1988). This bias may encourage isolation from the majority population as well as from members of one's own cultural group. For example, considerable stigma is attached to a disability in Hispanic and Asian-American cultures; these negative perceptions may cause persons with disabilities to internalize maladaptive views about their abilities or aspirations. The severity of a disability also may influence isolation because the impact of a disability on adjustment, functioning, and social isolation increases as the disability becomes more severe (Hardman, Drew, Egan, & Wolf, 1990). When a woman has a disability, the chances of isolation and stereotyping from the general population and one's own cultural circle become even greater and more complex (Alston & McCowan, 1994).

Family Responsibilities

Minority populations, particularly women, may experience a higher probability of having family responsibilities that interfere with successful vocational rehabilitation. Gottfredson (1986) pointed out that the responsibility of being a caregiver typically is assumed to be a career problem for women but is much more prevalent among women in some racial/ethnic groups than in others. African- and Hispanic-American women are likely to have more children at younger ages than women in other cultural groups (Gottfredson, 1986). The early presence of children may interfere significantly with the ability to explore career options and may force women to find immediate employment to care for their children.

The career behavior of men from minority groups also may be at risk because of family responsibilities. Hispanic-American men are more likely than white American men to be sole economic providers; African-American men are less likely to be primary economic providers. Brooks (1980) noted that many men from minority groups experience restricted career choices because they are less free to seek self-fulfillment in roles that do not produce income, or they experience pressure to find employment that is culturally acceptable or expected.

Impact of Risk Factors on Career Choice and Development

The potential impact of identified risk factors can be classified into four career-related problems: lack of self-knowledge, conflicting life goals and values, career goals and values that conflict with significant others, and perceived barriers to opportunity (Gottfredson, 1986).

1. *Lack of self-knowledge*: This career-choice problem can be traced to the social and cultural isolation that often accompanies the dual status of the minority and disabled. These statuses can restrict one's opportunities and experiences in developing and attempting career-related interests and competencies.

2. *Conflicting life goals and values (internal conflict)*: A lack of knowledge about one's vocational interests and aptitudes may lead to difficulty in identifying appropriate career goals or to an inability to reconcile incompatible career goals. This type of problem

often is compounded for persons who are the primary economic provider or those who hold career interests considered nontraditional.

3. *Career goals and values that conflict with significant others (external conflict)*: Many people from minority populations with disabilities may pursue occupations that they are either unsuited for or uninterested in because their family and friends expect them to be employed in areas that are typical for their gender, race, ethnic group, social class, or particular family tradition.

4. *Perceived barriers to opportunity*: Clients from minority backgrounds are more likely to limit their employment search and less likely to solicit assistance from rehabilitation services because of perceived barriers to particular job opportunities (Gottfredson, 1986). Whether real or not, clients' perceptions of employment barriers and opportunities may result in their pursuing jobs that are of little interest to them simply because they perceive these jobs as being readily available. (A detailed description of the risk framework and career problems is provided by Gottfredson [1986]).

Ultimately, the impact of being at risk can be seen in the higher rates of unemployment and underemployment in minority populations. Restrictive employment patterns are well documented and reveal that members of a minority group are more likely to enter culturally traditional areas representing lower-level social, enterprising, or conventional interests and activities (Arbona & Novy, 1991; Dunn & Veltman, 1989). Unfortunately, similar patterns are reflected in the rehabilitation outcomes of clients from minority groups, who are underrepresented in the rehabilitation delivery system, have not accessed rehabilitation services as readily — or received the same quality of service — as white Americans, and are more likely to have a case closed for being uncooperative (Wright, 1988).

IMPLICATIONS AND SUGGESTIONS FOR PRACTICE

The values, beliefs, and world views of different cultures should influence the way rehabilitation services are provided. Although it is critical that counselors respond to challenges presented by diverse populations, understanding the impact of cultural differences on rehabilitation needs and providing appropriate services that address these needs are not easy tasks.

Self-Appraisal of Personal World Views:

The first step in being an effective cross-cultural counselor is to develop an awareness of one's own world views, including personal biases, stereotypes, and an awareness of diverse groups in our society, and to understand how these views relate to perceptions of vocational opportunities for clients from minority backgrounds (Herbert & Cheatham, 1988). This is an important step because identifying individual values may help clarify similarities and differences with the values held by members of other cultures.

Assessment of one's personal world view includes a series of questions about whether one has a collective or individual orientation, competitive or collaborative approach to task completion, is people oriented or task oriented, and lives with a small nuclear family or has a large extended family network. Counselors should honestly assess their stereotypes, biases, or prejudices, as well as possible ways that these views may influence the delivery of counseling services to all types of clients. Counselors also may want to evaluate the practice of their office or agency staff toward minority clients. The number of referrals or applications, drop-out or unsuccessful closure rates, client satisfaction, and the provision or availability of appropriate services for minority clients may be assessed to identify areas in need of improvement.

Although merely thinking about cultural beliefs is not enough, it is a necessary first step in the process of developing cultural sensitivity (Ridley, Mendoza, Kanitz, Angermeier, & Zenk, 1994). Effective vocational rehabilitation for culturally diverse clients requires a respect for the world views of others and nonjudgmental understanding of the impact these diverse views have on each step of the rehabilitation process. This is by no means an easy task and may cause problems or dilemmas. Case in point: Is it unethical to label a behavior as maladaptive if that behavior is common in a client's culture? A full treatment of this question is subject to a debate that is beyond the scope of this chapter. However, if counselors respect and are sensitive to the cultural views of diverse groups, labeling such a behavior as maladaptive would be unethical; it would impose the status quo view that different behaviors and beliefs found in diverse groups represent genetic or cultural deficiencies that must be changed.

Recently, competencies and standards were proposed for multicultural counseling that consist of three areas – personal awareness, cultural awareness, and appropriate intervention and skills (Sue et al., 1992).

Initial Intake Interview and Goal Setting:

The need to consider the potential impact of cultural diversity on rehabilitation counseling has immediate pertinence at the start of therapy. Therefore, such consideration should begin during the initial intake interview and continue throughout subsequent meetings. Given the complexity of cultural identity, the types and severity of risk factors experienced, racial identity, and level of acculturation should be considered. Knowledge about these three factors will help determine the impact of culture on a client's behavior, career preference, and involvement in the rehabilitation process. Clients with limited levels of acculturation will be more likely to adhere to traditional cultural world views; clients with greater levels of acculturation will accept or adopt more of the mainstream culture's views and beliefs. Similarly, a client in the resistance stage of racial identity may mistrust the entire rehabilitation system because it represents the dominant culture. Knowledge about racial identity could be used to explain why a client displays noncompliant or hostile behavior toward the counselor. Once identified and understood, this information can be used in developing appropriate rehabilitation goals and interventions.

Other information that counselors may want to gather from potential clients may include their language preference, generational status (i.e., immigration history or years of residence in the United States), locus of control, and cultural orientation or preferences. Individual, family, and cultural views about disabilities also should be determined, especially for clients whose cultures may have negative views about disabilities. Counselors should consider general cultural values and beliefs, such as the types of behaviors valued by their client's culture, appropriate child-rearing practices, and notions of "proper" mental or physical health.

Questions can be directed toward the client and family to determine their understanding and opinion with regard to the disability. Topics for discussion should include the perceived role of the supernatural in causing disabilities, causes of illness, the perceptions of significant others toward the person with the disability, and ideas about the various roles of people in our society (deMateo-Smith, 1987; Leung, 1987; Mardiros, 1989). Through this type of questioning, rehabilitation counselors can determine the unique impact of a client's culture on occupational goals, prognosis for employment (including potential difficulties or conflicts between individual cultural values and those of local area employers), and special considerations that might be needed in the rehabilitation plan (e.g., an interpreter, classes in English as a second language, types of suitable employment options, and willingness or ability to work in conflicting cultural environments).

As a result of cultural beliefs regarding persons with disabilities, receipt of assistance from outsiders, or mistrust of services provided by the dominant culture, many persons from minority backgrounds in need of rehabilitation services may go unnoticed without *sustained* community outreach efforts. Counselors must understand the importance of contacting prospective clients in their homes or at other places where they feel comfortable. Atkinson and colleagues (1993, p. 300) described the benefits associated with outreach efforts:

> By making (themselves) available in the client's environment, the counselor is in a better position to respond to client needs at the time they are experienced. Exposure to the client's world may also help the counselor understand the cultural experience of the client and may enhance the counselor-client relationship.

Vocational Assessment:

Vocational assessment traditionally has played a significant role in the rehabilitation process. Because of the pivotal nature of assessment, it is important to consider the potential bias inherent in many standardized tests and to ensure that culturally appropriate assessment tools and procedures are used (Smart & Smart, 1993). Fouad (1993) notes that the role of vocational assessment is heavily influenced by dominant American culture, which emphasizes verbal communication, individuality, and a rational linear decision-making process. Likewise, the development and use of standardized vocational assessment instruments also reflect these values. Thus, as differences between a client's cultural values and mainstream values increase, greater caution must be exercised in interpreting results. Counselors can use a client's level of acculturation to measure this disparity.

Each instrument used in the assessment process should be examined for reliability, validity, and availability of comparable norm groups. Counselors should question whether instruments acknowledge the role of behavior in different cultures, the meanings attached to behavior and concepts, the degree to which an instrument measures the same construct in different cultures, and the precision of instrument translation for clients who are not proficient in the English language (Fouad, 1993).

Local norms may be established for different cultural groups for the tests and assessments commonly used to determine interests and aptitudes. The process of establishing local norms can be fairly lengthy and involved. However, this information can contribute to a more realistic appraisal of a client's interests and aptitudes and support better-informed decision making.

General Counseling Issues:

Is the rehabilitation process different for clients from minority backgrounds? The literature on this topic presents two contrasting perspectives. One perspective maintains that the career counseling and rehabilitation process should be the same for everyone regardless of cultural orientation. The opposing view suggests that the process should be very different for clients from minority groups. Leong (1993) suggests that the truth probably lies somewhere in between these two positions.

CLIENT CLARIFICATION OF THE IMPACT OF CULTURE

Clients from minority backgrounds may need guidance in developing self-identity, career goals, or the steps necessary to achieve these goals. They must consider and understand how their culture, race, disability, racial identity, or level of acculturation influences the types of career choice alternatives they view as acceptable. Clients may subscribe to cultural stereotypes about acceptable occupations or be unwilling to pursue occupations that promote conflicting cultural values. These views may result in lowered career aspirations and a sense of diminished choices.

Throughout the rehabilitation process, counselors must be aware that self-disclosure may be difficult and foreign, if not impossible, for some clients due to their cultural beliefs. If this is encountered, the counselor may ask the client to become a "cultural informant" and share general information about his or her cultural beliefs and values. In this manner, clients will reveal their own beliefs and values without being forced into self-disclosure (Leung, 1987).

GOAL SETTING

Culture may influence a client's expectations of and behavior during the rehabilitation process, particularly as it relates to goal setting. A determination should be made early as to the client's preference for a structured, directive counseling approach as opposed to an open-ended, nondirective approach (Bowman, 1993). Minority group members may prefer immediate goals and action-oriented approaches and may have different time perspectives than the majority culture (Sue & Sue, 1990). In addition, some cultures (e.g., Asian and Native American) have a more extrinsic and practical view of careers than the dominant culture and may not be interested in viewing a career as an issue of self-concept or self-actualization (Leong, 1993). This knowledge is extremely valuable because it will dictate not only the types of careers explored but also the approaches used.

Other aspects of the goal-setting process also may be affected by a person's culture. Many minority cultures possess a collective perspective that may compel counselors (or others) to permit, even encourage, family members to become involved in the rehabilitation process. This involvement should capitalize on the support and reinforcement provided by a client's extended family network. It may be a necessity for younger clients or for those who experience low levels of acculturation and high familial bonds (Hawks & Muha, 1991). Another benefit of involving others is that the client's problem can be viewed in the larger context of the extended family.

The goal-setting process should respect the values and beliefs of diverse cultures. Respect may be shown through verbal and nonverbal communication appropriate for the client's culture. Use of the client's primary language, especially if it is different from English, also will signal respect and support for minority clients. The value system of the client must be included in the goal-setting process. Also, the counselor must be sensitive to the client's spiritual values and the values of his or her family and religious organization (Wilson & Stith, 1991). Other actions — for example, not scheduling a meeting on a cultural holiday or during an important religious celebration — may seem obvious but, believe it or not, frequently are overlooked.

At some point, most rehabilitation counselors will encounter situations in which a client's cultural values significantly limit occupational alternatives. Should attempts be made to change clients' cultural values to enhance their employability or should counselors support and affirm cultural beliefs realizing that employability options may be limited? One might argue that it is best for minority clients to assimilate into the dominant culture; in doing so, potential employment problems could be avoided (Leong, 1993). However, using assimilation as a rehabilitation strategy devalues cultural diversity and adopts a culturally superior attitude toward clients from different backgrounds. Thus, I would argue that other approaches to this dilemma should be considered.

Some clients may be able to retain their cultural values and still function competently in the dominant culture. Clients who are socialized, comfortable, and effective in both dominant and minority cultures are considered "bicultural." Counselors can determine a client's level of biculturalism by assessing the degree of cultural overlap; availability of cultural translators, mediators, and models; corrective feedback regarding attempts at normative behavior; compatibility of the client's conceptual style with the style valued by the dominant culture; the client's degree of bilingualism; and the degree of dissimilarity in physical appearance between the client and those representative of the dominant culture (Atkinson et al., 1993). Problems may exist if clients are viewed as being bicultural when, in fact, they are actually marginal (caught between two cultures with little or no allegiance to either one). Therefore, caution must be taken when assessing a client's level of bicultural competence.

Some clients' cultural values may clash with those found in the dominant culture. Rather than attempting to change cultural values or beliefs, counselors should increase their clients' awareness of how their cultural orientation affects available employment options. Disparities should be discussed openly. Alternative employment options can be identified that support, or at least do not conflict with, a client's cultural values, which may mean the availability of fewer or less desirable jobs. Even so, counselors can best serve their minority clients by exploring available options, discussing possible outcomes of the client's alternatives factually rather than normatively, and then providing counseling support so that the client can reach an informed decision.

ADVOCACY

Counselors must acknowledge the importance of being an advocate—a change agent—for minority clients. Advocacy starts with the recognition that many problems experienced by a person from a minority group result from the system rather than flaws inherent within the client. Counselors should help clients identify situations where problems are caused by external forces and find ways to eliminate or reduce the effects of these forces; for example, educating local area employers about oppressive hiring practices or discriminatory employee attitudes (Hawks & Muha, 1991).

Advocacy seems especially important during job placement when sensitivity to sociological aspects of work also must be considered. Smart and Smart (1993, p. 168) encouraged rehabilitation counselors to "[b]ecome aware of restrictive social conditions, prejudices, and discrimination, which work against those people who are both in a minority and have a disability. The social environment, including discrimination, lack of opportunity, and culturally biased assumptions imposed by the broader culture, have built formidable barriers to job placement."

Thus, job placement must be tempered with an awareness of inequities in the system and should address issues of empowerment and entitlement in the workplace. Of course, sometimes counselors must reign in their advocacy and recognize the appropriate distinction between sociopolitical action and working with clients in counseling; for example, it is important to avoid making any client a "trailblazer" (i.e., the first minority worker with a disability who will pave the way for future hirings).

CONCLUSION

Attaining cultural competence is a continuous process of raising one's awareness of personal assumptions and world views of becoming aware of and empathizing with the world views of clients from culturally diverse backgrounds, and then developing and practicing appropriate, relevant, and sensitive intervention strategies and skills for them. Undoubtedly, this process will continue to change over time — as the values and beliefs of separate cultures change in response to the influence of one another, the ideas and experiences of ensuing generations, and the dominant culture. This underscores the point that "becoming culturally sensitive is an active process, that is ongoing, and that it is a process that never reaches an end point" (Sue & Sue, 1990, p. 146).

REFERENCES

Alston, R. J., & McCowan, C. J. (1994). African-American women with disabilities: Rehabilitation issues and concerns. *Journal of Rehabilitation, 60*, 36–40.

Anderson, D., Wang, J., & Houser, R. (1993). Issues and needs of persons with disabilities in Hawaii: An exploration of racial/ethnic group differences. *Journal of Rehabilitation, 59*, 11–16.

Arbona, C., & Novy, D. M. (1991). Career aspirations and expectations of Black, Mexican American, and White students. *Career Development Quarterly, 39*, 231–239.

Atkins, B. J. (1992). Transition for individuals who are culturally diverse. In F. R. Rusch, L. DeStefano, J. Chadsey-Rusch, L. A. Phelps, & E. Szymanski (Eds.), *Transition from school to adult life: Models, linkages, and policy* (pp. 443–458). Sycamore, IL: Sycamore Publishing.

Atkins, B. J., & Wright, T. J. (1980). Vocational rehabilitation of blacks. *Journal of Rehabilitation, 46*(2), 40–46.

Atkinson, D. R., Morten, G., & Sue, D. W. (1993). *Counseling American minorities: A cross-cultural perspective* (4th ed.). Dubuque, IA: Wm. C. Brown Communications.

Bowman, S. L. (1993). Career intervention strategies for ethnic minorities. *Career Development Quarterly, 42*, 14–25.

Brooks, L. (1980). Recent developments in theory building. In D. Brown & L. Brooks (Eds.), *Career choice and development: Applying contemporary theories to practice* (2nd ed., pp. 364–394). San Francisco, CA: Jossey-Bass.

Brown, D. (1990). Issues and trends in career development: Theory and practice. In D. Brown & L. Brooks (Eds.), *Career choice and development* (2nd ed., pp. 506–518). San Francisco, CA: Jossey-Bass.

Clark, S., & Kelly, S. D. M. (1992). Traditional Native American values: Conflict or concordance in rehabilitation? *Journal of Rehabilitation, 58*, 23–28.

Comas-Diaz, L. (1993). Hispanic Latino communities: Psychological implications. In D. R. Atkinson, G. Morten, & D. W. Sue (Eds.), *Counseling American minorities: A cross-cultural perspective* (4th ed., pp. 245-263). Dubuque, IA: William C. Brown Communications.

Correa, V. I. (1987). Working with Hispanic parents of visually impaired children: Cultural implications. *Journal of Visual Impairment and Blindness, 81,* 260-264.

Cross, W. E., Jr. (1994). Nigrescence theory: Historical and explanatory notes. *Journal of Vocational Behavior, 44,* 119-123.

deMateo-Smith, R. (1987). *Multicultural considerations: Working with families of developmentally disabled and high risk children. The Hispanic perspective.* (ERIC Document Reproduction Service No. ED 285 358). Los Angeles: National Center for Clinical Infant Programs.

Dunn, C. W., & Veltman, G. C. (1989). Addressing the restrictive career maturity patterns of minority youth: A program evaluation. *Journal of Multicultural Counseling and Development, 17,* 156-164.

Evans, K. M., & Herr, E. L. (1944). The influence of racial identity and the perception of discrimination on the career aspirations of African American men and women. *Journal of Vocational Behavior, 44,* 173-184.

Fouad, N. A. (1993). Cross-cultural vocational assessment. *Career Development Quarterly, 42,* 4-13.

Garza, R. (1986). Socioeconomic and cultural problems affecting the delivery of rehabilitation services to Hispanic blind and visually disabled individuals—some observations. In S. Walker, F. Z. Belgrave, A. M. Banner, & R. W. Nicholls (Eds.), *Equal to the challenge: Perspectives, problems, and strategies in the rehabilitation of the nonwhite disabled.* Washington, DC: Howard University.

Gottfredson, L. S. (1986). Special groups and the beneficial use of vocational interest inventories. In W. B. Walsh, S. H. Osipow (Eds.), *Advances in vocational psychology, volume I: The assessment of interests* (pp. 127-198). Hillsdale, NJ: Lawrence Erlbaum Associates.

Hardman, M. L., Drew, C. J., Egan, M. W., & Wolf, B. (1990). *Human exceptionality: Society, school, and family* (4th ed.). Boston: Allyn & Bacon.

Hawks, B. K., & Muha, D. (1991). Facilitating the career development of minorities: Doing it differently this time. *Career Development Quarterly, 39,* 251–260.

Helms, J. E. (1984). Toward a theoretical explanation of the effects of race on counseling: A black and white model. *Counseling Psychologist, 12,* 153–164.

Helms, J. E., & Piper R. E. (1994). Implications of racial identity theory for vocational psychology. *Journal of Vocational Behavior, 44,* 124–138.

Herbert, J. T., & Cheatham, H. E. (1988). Africentricity and the black disability experience: A theoretical orientation of rehabilitation counselors. *Journal of Applied Rehabilitation Counseling, 19,* 50–54.

Jenkins, A. E., & Amos, O. C. (1983). Being black and disabled: A pilot study. *Journal of Rehabilitation, 49,* 54–60.

Kutscher, R. E. (1990). *Outlook 2000.* (Bulletin No. 2352, pp. 65-73). Washington, DC: Bureau of Labor Statistics.

LaFromboise, T. D. (1980). American Indian mental health policy. *American Psychologist, 43,* 388–397.

LaFromboise, T. D., Trimble, J. E., & Mohatt, G. V. (1990). Counseling intervention and American Indian tradition: An integrative approach. *Counseling Psychologist, 18,* 628–652.

Leong, F. T. L. (1991). Career development attributes and occupational values of Asian American and White American college students. *Career Development Quarterly, 39,* 221–230.

Leong, F. T. L. (1993). The career counseling process with racial-ethnic minorities: The case of Asian Americans. *Career Development Quarterly, 42,* 26–40.

Leong, F. T. L., & Chou, E. L. (1994). The role of ethnic identity and acculturation in the vocational behavior of Asian Americans: An integrative review. *Journal of Vocational Behavior, 44,* 155–172.

Leung, B. (1987). *Cultural considerations in working with Asian parents.* (ERIC Document Reproduction Service No. ED 285 359). Los Angeles: National Center for Clinical Infant Programs.

Leung, P., & Sakata, R. (1988). Asian Americans and rehabilitation: Some important variables. *Journal of Applied Rehabilitation Counseling, 19,* 16-20.

Leung, S. A. (1993). Circumscription and compromise: A replication study with Asian Americans. *Journal of Counseling Psychology, 40,* 188-193.

LoneWolf-Miller, D., & Joe, J. R. (1993). Employment barriers and work motivation for Navajo rehabilitation clients. *International Journal of Rehabilitation Research, 16,* 107-117.

Luzzo, D. A. (1992). Ethnic group and social class differences in college students' career development. *Career Development Quarterly, 41,* 161-173.

Mardiros, M. (1989). Conception of childhood disability among Mexican-American parents. *Medical Anthropology, 12,* 55-68.

Marion, R. L. (1980). Communicating with parents of culturally diverse exceptional children. *Exceptional Children, 46,* 616-623.

Martin, W. E., Jr. (1991). Career development and American Indians living on reservations: Cross-cultural factors to consider. *Career Development Quarterly, 39,* 273-283.

Morrow, R. D. (1987). Cultural differences—Be aware! *Academic Therapy, 23,* 143-149.

Parham, T. J., & Austin, N. L. (1994). Career development and African Americans: A contextual reappraisal using the Nigrescence construct. *Journal of Vocational Behavior, 44,* 139-154.

Ridley, C. R., Mendoza, D. W., Kanitz, B. E., Angermeier, L.,& Zenk, R. (1994). Cultural sensitivity in multicultural counseling: A perceptual schema model. *Journal of Counseling Psychology, 41,* 125-136.

Smart, J. F., & Smart, D. W. (1990). Cultural issues in the rehabilitation of Hispanics. *Journal of Rehabilitation, 58,* 29-37.

Smart, J. F., & Smart, D. W. (1993). The rehabilitation of Hispanics with disabilities: Sociocultural constraints. *Rehabilitation Education, 7,* 167-184.

Smith, E. J. (1980). Career development of minorities in nontraditional fields. *Journal of Non-White Concerns and Personnel Guidance, 8,* 141-156.

Sue, D. W., Arredondo, P., & McDavis, R. J. (1992). Multicultural counseling competencies and standards: A call to the profession. *Journal of Multicultural Counseling and Development, 20,* 64–88.

Sue, D. W., & Sue, D. (1990). *Counseling the culturally different* (2nd ed.). New York: John Wiley & Sons.

Swanson, J. L. (1993). Integrating a multicultural perspective into training for career counseling: Programmatic and individual interventions. *Career Development Quarterly, 42,* 41–49.

Thomason, T. C. (1991). Counseling Native Americans: An introduction for non-Native American counselors. *Journal of Counseling and Development, 69,* 321–327.

Tinsley, H. E. A. (1994). Racial identity and vocational behavior. *Journal of Vocational Behavior, 44,* 115–117.

Turner, A. (1987). *Multicultural considerations: Working with families of developmentally disabled and high risk children. The black perspective.* (ERIC Document Reproduction Service No. ED 285 360). Los Angeles: National Center for Clinical Infant Programs.

Wilson, L. L., & Stith, S. M. (1991). Culturally sensitive therapy with Black clients. *Journal of Multicultural Counseling and Development, 19,* 32–43.

Wright, T. J. (1988). Enhancing the professional preparation of rehabilitation counselors for improved services to ethnic minorities with disabilities. *Journal of Applied Rehabilitation Counseling, 19,* 4–10.

11

Vocational Evaluation of Hispanic Clients with Disabilities

Julie F. Smart, PhD, CRC, NCC, LPC, ABDA, and David W. Smart, PhD

Dr. Julie Smart is Assistant Professor, Department of Special Education and Rehabilitation, Utah State University, Logan, UT. Dr. David Smart is Professor, Counseling and Development Center, Brigham Young University, Provo, UT.

KEY POINTS

- Because of language and acculturation differences, Hispanic clients may present unique challenges to the vocational evaluator that may not be found with white American clients. In addition, vocational evaluation may be more difficult with Hispanic clients than with other American ethnic minorities because of Hispanics' strong language loyalty.

- It is the vocational evaluator's task to work *with* such diversity rather than *against* it. Although initially more time consuming and expensive, thorough and ac-

curate multicultural rehabilitation evaluations are more economical in the long run.

- This chapter presents five problematic areas in the vocational evaluation of Hispanic clients: difficulty in defining Hispanic populations, inequitable employee selection, test content that is foreign to Hispanic culture, inappropriate standardization samples on tests, and language bias. Possible solutions and recommendations for practice are outlined for each area.

Some of this chapter appeared in: Smart, J. F., & Smart, D. W. (1993). Vocational evaluation of Hispanics with disabilities: Issues and implications. Vocational Evaluation and Work Adjustment Bulletin, 26, *111–122.*

INTRODUCTION

Persons of minority backgrounds often exhibit behaviors and attitudes that have previously not been measured. Because of language and acculturation differences, Hispanic clients may present unique challenges to the vocational evaluator that may not be found with white American clients (Arnold & Orozco, 1987, 1989; Linskey, Arnold, & Hancock, 1983; Smart & Smart, 1992a, 1992b). Vocational evaluation may be more difficult with Hispanic clients than with other American ethnic minorities because of Hispanics' strong language loyalty; more than other cultural and ethnic minorities, Hispanic persons have continued to use their native language, Spanish.

It is the vocational evaluator's task to work *with* such diversity rather than *against* it. In the short run, it may be more challenging to accept and work with the complexity of multicultural evaluations; however, when vocational evaluators are successful in meeting this challenge, clients are more likely to enjoy a higher quality of life and make their optimal contributions through their work. Thus, although initially more time consuming and expensive, thorough and accurate multicultural rehabilitation evaluations are really more economical in the long run.

Vocational evaluation rests on the assumption that a sample of a client's behavior can be used to predict future job performance. For this prediction to be accurate, the behavioral sample should represent the client's best performance and incorporate a number of opportunities for the client to exhibit knowledge and skills in a wide variety of domains. This chapter presents five problematic areas in the vocational evaluation of Hispanic clients and outlines possible solutions and recommendations for practice.

DEFINING HISPANIC POPULATIONS

As census takers and other demographers are learning, it is

difficult to assign an exact definition to the status of "Hispanic" (Arbona, 1990; Cataeno, 1986; Duran, 1989; Fradd & Correa, 1989; Leal, 1990; Moore; 1990; Shorris; 1992; Smart, 1993; Winkler, 1990; Wodarski, 1991). The term *Hispanic* did not exist before the 1970 census (Davis, Haub, & Willette, 1983). Is such status defined by race, ethnicity, language skill, language preference, level of acculturation, nation of origin, surname, or self-identification? These issues are important in vocational evaluation because the Spanish translation of a test such as the Minnesota Multiphasic Personality Inventory (MMPI) may be quite different for a Puerto Rican client than for a Mexican-American client. To be sure, the validity of the vocational evaluation may be greatly influenced by the evaluator's degree of sensitivity to the characteristics of the particular Hispanic subgroup to which the client belongs.

Puente (1990) stated:

> The WAIS [Wechsler Adult Intelligence Scale] has also been translated and standardized with Puerto Rican populations (1980). It was assumed that all translations would be appropriate; this assumption, however, is incorrect.
>
> Puerto Rican, Chicano, Mexican, Latin American, South American, and Castilian Spanish not only have their own dialects and idiosyncrasies but in many cases, their own language. Thus, the Puerto Rican translation of the WAIS has limited usefulness with non-Puerto Rican subjects. Further, though yet to be researched, the issue of norms needs to be addressed. For example, Puerto Rican norms may differ from Argentinian norms. (p. 513)

Another important consideration in carefully defining the various Hispanic subgroups is underscored by the fact that they may differ in their average test scores. The literature points to differences among various Hispanic subgroups in the manner in which they perform on tests of academic ability (Schmitt, 1988; Schmitt & Dorans, 1991). Because of the consistent differences among Mexican Americans, Puerto Ricans, and other persons of Hispanic origin, the College Board and the American College Testing Program now report three separate "within ethnic" scores for Hispanic persons on the Scholastic Aptitude Test (SAT) and the American College Test (ACT) (Schmitt & Dorans, 1991). This policy speaks to the need for rehabilitation counselors to be sensitive to possible cultural differences among Hispanic subgroups when conducting evaluations.

Recommendations for Practice:

The most valid and accurate process of determining a client's identification is simply to ask him or her. This process of self-identification should include such information as country of origin, the experience of migration, generational status in the United States, language skill and preferences, level of education in both English and Spanish, and self-assessment of acculturation level. Vocational counselors may find it helpful to use a formalized measure of acculturation to understand some clients more fully. The most widely accepted acculturation inventories for Hispanic clients are those developed by Cuellar and colleagues (1980) and Szapocznik and associates (1978). The meaning of the scores of these measures, which are easy to administer and can be completed quickly, is straightforward and simple to understand.

In addition, vocational counselors should note the sample of the population on whom various tests have been used. Accurate interpretations of test scores can be extended only to those groups that have been included in the norming sample. Lists of the normative groups generally can be found in the test manuals accompanying each test. Care should be taken to identify and use tests that have been used on Hispanic groups.

INEQUITABLE EMPLOYEE SELECTION

Eyde (1992) stated, "By the year 2000, Hispanic clients. . . and other minority groups are expected to make up one third of the new entrants into the labor force" (p. 167). Therefore, the issue of equitable employee selection is becoming increasingly pressing. The National Commission on Testing and Public Policy (1990) noted that because of the fallibility and imprecision of tests, and the criterion measures on which they are based, *fewer* minority persons who *could* perform successfully on the job are actually selected. This is defined as inequitable employee selection. The unfortunate consequence of such imprecise tests is that the full range of a client's knowledge, skills, and aptitudes is not recognized. Thus, basing selection decisions exclusively on test performance often will result in selecting a nonminority candidate (Campos, 1989; Ramos, 1981, 1992). In such an instance, the practical impact ("utility" in psychometric terms) of this specific selection may hurt the minority group member, who may have been repeatedly passed over for jobs (Camara, 1992; Zeidner, 1988). It should be noted, however, that in the psychometric literature, much evidence suggests that for members of the majority culture, tests more accurately reflect abilities and aptitudes (Gatewood & Perloff, 1990).

Because vocational evaluation is, by definition, behavior oriented and is based on direct measures of various skills and behaviors, it offers the hope of objectivity and accuracy, which may not be found in other types of assessment. Vocational evaluation, which is conducted in settings that closely approximate the natural work setting and which is heavily outcome oriented, is potentially less biased than assessment procedures that rely solely on psychological and personality constructs.

Another potential advantage of vocational evaluation is the fact that it is directly linked to both treatment and outcome; therefore, it is useful for rehabilitation counselors and helpful for clients. Because the client is directly involved in behaviors and work sample procedures that are similar to those in the job setting, motivation is increased.

The breadth, diversity, and comprehensiveness of the evaluations represent additional positive aspects of vocational evaluation, which offers the promise of equal employment. When these aspects are incorporated into vocational evaluations and used in rehabilitation, the outcomes are more likely to be culturally fair (American Psychological Association of Ethnic Minority Affairs, 1993; Eyde, Moreland, Robertson, Primoff, & Most, 1988; Primoff & Eyde, 1988). For example, vocational counselors have long known that the value of intelligence tests goes far beyond the simple, single numerical IQ score. Such tests provide a rich source of information about a client's cognitive processes, problem-solving abilities, thinking patterns, and language skills.

Recommendations for Practice:

Use of situational analysis provides a richer profile of a client's abilities and strengths. Behavioral observations should include:

- Quality and quantity of output

- Distractibility during a task

- Avoidance of an activity

- Requests for assistance

- Spatial or sequential pattern of response

- Frustration tolerance

- Response delays

- Self-corrections

- Need for encouragement and instruction

- Record-keeping skills

- Strategies used

- Ability to learn from demonstration

- Task presentation preference

- Use of investigative behavior

- Communication abilities

- Willingness to ask relevant questions

Another valid and potentially useful evaluation technique is to link job placement with the client's learning style. (Both the Learning Style Inventory and the Myers Briggs Type Indicator have been translated into Spanish.)

Three factors should be considered when using situational and behavioral analyses in vocational evaluation. First, behavioral analysis should be used in conjunction with standardized, quantitative psychometric data. Second, the indices of difficulty should be described in detail. Third, the counselor should be aware that whenever nonstandard approaches are implemented, psychometric properties are violated.

INAPPROPRIATE TEST CONTENT

There are numerous examples of test items that tap into knowledge domains that are foreign to the cultures of Hispanic persons (Berry, 1972, 1983; Duran, 1989; Lonner, 1985; Smart & Smart, 1993; Valencia & Rankin, 1985; Watkins & Campbell, 1990). Including such items in intelligence, personality, or achievement tests introduces a bias that reduces the test's validity for Hispanic persons. Examples of such bias include asking questions about the seasons to someone who lives in the tropics, using pictures of a European-style nutcracker, and asking for the name of the president of the United States.

Many examples regarding test items that are not "culturally fair" can be cited (Berry, 1972; Butcher, 1984; Butcher & Garcia, 1978; Butcher & Pancheri, 1976; Cattell, 1940; Chavez & Gonzales-Singh, 1980; Cole, 1981; Dahlstrom, Lachar, & Dahlstrom, 1986; Malgady, Rogler, & Constantino, 1987; Montgomery & Orozco, 1985; Padilla, Olmedo, & Loya, 1987; Padilla & Ruiz, 1973; Ramos, 1992; Sandoval, 1979; Sundberg & Gonzales, 1981; Thorndike, 1971; Violato, 1984). "All tests are 'anchored' in an originating culture or culture area (e.g., Latin America, but usually the United States) and are therefore 'unfair' (or at least not as 'meaningful') to people who reside in another culture or who belong to an ethnic minority group" (Lonner, 1985, p. 601). Two such examples are the Weschler Adult Intelligence Scale-Revised (WAIS-R) and The Peabody Picture Vocabulary Test (PPVT). In the WAIS-R, it was necessary to change eight items for Canadian testing populations to make the test more sensitive and reflective of Canadian culture (Violato, 1984). The PPVT, considered by many experts to be relatively "culture free" or at least "culture reduced" (Dunn & Dunn, 1981), contains many pictures that were at odds with the way these items were perceived in Great Britain. Given the linguistic and cultural *similarities* among Canada, Great Britain, and the United States — as well as their common history and intellectual traditions — vocational evaluations should reflect the more obvious *differences* that must be bridged when assessing Hispanic clients, whose language and customs are vastly different from those shared by Anglo Americans.

Test items reflect the knowledge and experience of the culture in which they are developed. Cultural bias occurs when these tests are translated to another culture because the connotation of a word in one language may be slightly different from that in another language. The Vocabulary Test of the WAIS-R is a good example. The difficulty level of some of the items changes with the language used; although the difficulty level may be carefully validated in the United States, this may not be the case in Spanish-speaking countries.

Subtle changes from one culture to another often are overlooked when asking questions designed to measure comprehension and abstract reasoning abilities. For example, although a middle-class, white American would probably say it is better to give money to an organized charity than to a beggar (the "correct" response), this may not be the case with those who have recently migrated to the United States. In many countries, organized charities are known to be corrupt; thus, in many countries, begging may be an accepted part of the culture.

Even projective tests, such as the Rorschach Inkblot test, are not free of cultural influences (Kaplan, Rickers-Ovsiankina, & Joseph, 1956). Regarding the MMPI, an instrument often used in vocational evaluation, Velasquez and Callahan (1991) stated, "Because there is empirical evidence indicating that Hispanic clients may respond on the MMPI in a manner which may be interpreted as being indicative of greater psychopathology, we strongly recommend that clinicians integrate scale elevations with behavioral and observational correlates" (p. 261). Hispanic concepts of deity, such as beliefs about "God's presence," "His protection," and "His love," may contribute to the MMPI Dependence Scale and may distort the results in such a manner as to leave the impression that Hispanic persons are not as independent or self-directed as the norm groups in the broader American culture (American Psychological Association, 1985; Casas, 1985; Greene, 1987; Raven, Court, & Raven, 1985).

However, it should be recognized that numerous efforts have been made to create culture-free tests and improvements have been implemented (Darlington, 1971). Puente (1990) considered Cattell's attempt to factor out cultural bias in the Culture-Fair Intelligence Test to be the most significant effort to date in this regard (Darlington, 1971). One of Puente's criticisms, however, was the fact that Cattell's studies were performed on persons living in their own culture; Puente recommended that such attempts be made with minority persons residing in the United States.

Recommendations for Practice:

Of course, the question can be asked, "Are not persons of Hispanic origin seeking employment in the United States? Shouldn't Hispanic persons be able to compete on tests and in the workforce on a par with those who speak English and are native to the United States?" In answering these questions, we should keep in mind that an important part of vocational evaluation is assessing the *potential* of a client. Although some persons of Hispanic origin may not have immediate English language skills or knowledge of the culture, their potential abilities should be credited and recommendations made on the basis of these potentials. Tests such as the MMPI and the WAIS-R should not be completely abandoned but should be used with caution and only as one part of the evaluation. Employers' attitudes toward such tests vary depending on their intelligibility; the vocational counselor should be prepared to help employers understand and interpret test results.

INAPPROPRIATE STANDARDIZATION SAMPLES

Although test developers are becoming increasingly sensitive to the need to include appropriate samples of Hispanic persons and other minorities in the standardization samples, this has not always been the case (Figueroa, 1989; Holland, 1971, 1979; Ibrahim & Arredondo, 1986; Kuder & Diamond, 1979; Olmedo, 1977, 1981; Padilla & Lindholm, 1984). In some instances, the only Hispanic norms are clinical populations, thus invalidating the test for nonclinical Hispanic clients. Examples of clinical populations include those in prisons and mental hospitals. When clinical populations are the only minorities included in the standardization sample, the utility of the test is limited and the false stereotype of the maladaptive Hispanic person may be perpetuated. Even nonclinical Hispanic norms are of little value because of the great diversity among Hispanic subgroups (Zeidner, 1988).

It is of interest to note that surveys of occupational preference (Ortiz & Maldonado-Colon, 1986a, 1986b; Pennock-Roman, 1992; Rueda, 1989) have commonly separated the scales for men and women, but variables other than gender have not been accorded such attention. The Strong Interest Inventory is available in Spanish, but the composition of the standardization group is unclear, so it is highly probable that the standardization group did not speak Spanish.

Recommendations for Practice:

A person cannot accurately interpret normative test scores unless he or she has access to and understands information about the sample of people on whom the test was standardized. Therefore, a careful review of the test manual is essential to identify the standardization sample and the procedures by which it was obtained. If questions remain after having carefully read the manual, one may wish to consult unbiased reviews such as those published in the latest edition of the *Mental Measurements Yearbook* and *Tests in Print* (Buros, 1985; Murphy, Conoley, & Impara, 1994); such reviews evaluate tests and often review the standardization procedures.

If questions still remain, one may wish to contact the test publishers for additional information regarding the applicability of the test to the particular client(s) being evaluated. Test publishers are becoming increasingly sensitive to multicultural issues and are willing to cooperate with counselors who use their tests. In addition to uncovering more information about the standardization procedures, inquiries communicate to the publishing company and its technical staff that test users care about cultural diversity and that the quality of the test can be judged by its applicability to diverse groups.

Because test publishers are becoming more responsive to the needs of a pluralistic society, new editions of tests have been renormed to include samples of Hispanic persons. It follows, then, that due to these constant changes, the counselor should continually check newer test catalogues or call publishers for the latest updates and inquire about any renorming procedures that may be underway. Pricing discounts or prepublication use of tests may be available if an agency is willing to share the results of its evaluations as part of the publishers' renorming procedures.

Keep in mind that many subgroups and nationalities fall under the designation of Hispanic or Latino, and evaluators must be careful to interpret test results in light of these differences. The generalization of test results is most accurate when the nationality, socioeconomic status, educational level, age, gender, and language characteristics of the standardization sample are known.

In compiling the report of an evaluation, the evaluator should help the reader understand the meaning of the test scores in light of the standardization sample. If little similarity exists between client(s) being tested and the group on whom the test was normed, the clients should be cautioned about this. Because test scores are almost always presented in numerical form, these scores can assume an appearance of exactitude that may be misleading; therefore, it is the counselor's responsibility to provide an adequate explanation in his or her report so that the reader can evaluate the scores in light of the standardization procedures.

LANGUAGE BIAS

Many aspects of vocational evaluation depend on the use of language. Tests in a person's weaker language will underestimate his or her abilities (Goldman & Trueba, 1987). When modifications are made to minimize language dependence, subtle shifts begin to occur in evaluation, administration, scoring, and interpretation. Different languages have different facilities for encoding and manipulating particular types of materials (Ortiz & Maldonado-Colon, 1986a, 1986b). Even the format of the presentation of evaluation materials is critical.

Another language-related issue is that of carefully differentiating a disability from an English-language deficiency (Murphy, Conoley, & Impara, 1994). This is particularly important in the case of suspected disabilities such as developmental disabilities, visual and hearing losses, psychological disorders, and chronic mental illness (Anastasi, 1988). In these and other cases, it may be helpful to develop a carefully documented medical, mental, intellectual, and emotional history of the client apart from his or her language proficiencies.

Bilingualism, almost universally viewed as an advantage, must be reevaluated, because some cognate words (words that are spelled almost the same in both English and Spanish) are *false cognates* (words that sound alike but actually have totally different meanings) and others are *true cognates* (words that have similar or identical meanings) (Holland, 1979; Powers, 1982). Examples of false cognates include the Spanish word *exito*, which means success in Spanish (not exit); *pulpo*, which means octopus (not pulp); *caro*, which means expensive or beloved (not car); *fingir*, which means to pretend (not finger); and *embarrasada*, which means pregnant (not the commonly misinterpreted embarrassed). Therefore, on closer examination, bilingualism can be both an advantage and a disadvantage, depending on the vocabulary used in the vocational evaluation.

Pennock-Roman (1992) commented:

> Hence for some nonnative speakers having a low level of proficiency in the language of the test, scores on the test do not reflect the intended aptitude. Rather, low verbal-aptitude scores in a nonnative language reflect mostly examinees' limited proficiency in the language of the test. . . . If we consider persons at the extreme end with virtually no comprehension of the language of the test, we can predict that all would obtain randomly achieved, near-zero scores regardless of aptitude. (p. 102)

Furthermore, Anastasi (1988), the author of one of the most enduring (six editions) and respected texts on psychological testing, has observed that low IQ scores may simply mean low acculturation to the language and culture in which the test was given.

Recommendations for Practice:

A client's language dominance should be determined before the vocational evaluation. In which language is the client most proficient? Which is the client's first language? In which language(s) does the client read and write? Moreover, the language history of the client should be determined. What language did the client learn first? In which language(s) was the client educated? How did the client learn the second language? Estimates of the client's academic language ability in both Spanish and English are necessary.

Dual language testing should be used in some cases. This does not rule out testing in the client's weaker language, English. However, any dual testing techniques used should be carefully described in the vocational counselor's report.

Another rehabilitation issue involves the use of vocational evaluations conducted in the past. Although easy to access and economical in terms of time, effort, and money, previous vocational evaluations may not consider a client's newly acquired English-language skills.

The services of trained and supervised translators can be used. Training in vocational evaluation and psychometric techniques should be provided to translators. Such training should include cautions not to teach test material, not to provide inappropriate verbal and nonverbal cues, and not to allow extra time. The translator should simply read the instructions and the test items. A trained translator can also serve as a cultural consultant, explaining how certain responses are reasonable given the client's cultural background, although they would be scored as incorrect according to the test manual. Of course, use of a translator's services should be included in the vocational evaluator's report.

Finally, referral to a bilingual, bicultural vocational counselor should be considered when a client exhibits both a mild disability and low acculturation to the Anglo-American culture. In contrast to severe disabilities, mild disabilities and developmental disabilities may be difficult to distinguish from a lack of English language skills and acculturation. It is probably not necessary to refer *every* Hispanic client to a bilingual, bicultural vocational counselor; however, counselors should guard against having inappropriately low expectations of Hispanic clients.

GENERAL RECOMMENDATIONS FOR PRACTICE

Several final suggestions are in order. Hispanic clients — indeed all clients — should be given the opportunity to display what they know and what they can do. It is the obligation of the rehabilitation counselor and the vocational evaluator to provide the best conditions for testing and evaluation. Hispanic clients should be thoroughly oriented to the evaluation. Motivation and respect for the testing procedures should be encouraged by thoroughly describing what will occur and explaining the far-reaching effects of evaluation results. Many Hispanic clients do not understand the importance and use of such results.

In addition, test-taking skills should be taught. It is axiomatic that "test-wiseness" allows the test taker better to demonstrate his or her knowledge and abilities (Anastasi, 1988). Techniques such as ranking stimuli along a continuum, budgeting time, using the process of elimination, choosing only one correct response, and matching the question number with the item number on the answer sheet are examples of test-taking skills that can be taught to Hispanic clients before the evaluation begins.

Confidentiality guidelines should be communicated to the client to motivate self-disclosure on psychological and neuropsychological instruments. Respect for the client and his or her culture and language should be clearly communicated, and statements about the client's linguistic and cultural background should never be pejorative.

Culturally sensitive vocational evaluations will change the way in which reports are written and how they are used. Enough detail should be given for the users of the reports to understand what changes and additions were implemented in the evaluation. Was a certified, trained translator used? Was the order of administration changed? Have any standardized administration procedures been adapted? Were behavioral and situational assessments used? Other professionals will need to become accustomed to reading reports of alternative procedures. Solutions to such testing problems should be presented in written format with enough detail provided to describe the accommodations, adaptations, and overall objectives.

CONCLUSION

Although the issues and implications identified in this chapter may seem complex and drawn out — particularly in light of the heavy caseloads and constant pressure that vocational evaluators often experience — they are economical and practical in the long run. As the number of Hispanic clients increases, which it certainly will do, cultural sensitivity will ensure greater practicality and economy of effort as well as a higher standard of professional practice in vocational evaluation. Issues of culture and language affect the provision of these services and the profession must recognize this reality and adapt to it.

REFERENCES

American Psychological Association. (1985). *Standards for educational and psychological testing*. Washington, DC: Author.

American Psychological Association, Office of Ethnic Minority Affairs. (1993). Guidelines for providers of psychological services to ethnic, linguistic, and culturally diverse populations. *American Psychologist, 48,* 45–48.

Anastasi, A. (1988). *Psychological testing* (6th ed.). New York: Macmillan.

Arbona, C. (1990). Career counseling research and Hispanics: A review of the literature. *The Counseling Psychologist, 18,* 300–323.

Arnold, B. R., & Orozco, S. (1987). Acculturation and evaluation of disabled Mexican Americans. In B. R. Arnold (Ed.), *Disability, rehabilitation, and the Mexican American.* Edinburg, TX: Pan American University.

Arnold, B. R., & Orozco, S. (1989). Acculturation and evaluation of Mexican Americans with disabilities. *Journal of Rehabilitation, 55,* 53–57.

Berry, J. W. (1972). Radical cultural relativism and the concept of intelligence. In L. J. Cronbach & P. J. D. Drenth (Eds.), *Mental tests and cultural adaptations* (pp. 77–88). The Hague: Mounton.

Berry, J. W. (1983). Textured contexts: Systems and situations in cross-cultural psychology. In S. H. Irvine & J. W. Berry (Eds.), *Human assessment and cultural factors* (pp. 117–126). New York: Plenum Press.

Buros, O. K. (Ed.). (1985). *Mental measurements yearbook.* Highland Park, NJ: Gryphon.

Butcher, J. N. (1984). Current developments in MMPI use: An international perspective. In J. N. Butcher & C. D. Spielberger (Eds.), *Advances in personality assessment.* Hillsdale, NJ: Erlbaum.

Butcher, J. N., & Garcia, R. E. (1978). Cross-national application of psychological tests. *Personnel and Guidance Journal, 56,* 472–475.

Butcher, J. N., & Pancheri, P. (1976). *A handbook of cross-national MMPI research.* Minneapolis: University of Minnesota Press.

Camara, W. J. (1992). Fairness and fair use in employment testing: A matter of perspective. In K. F. Geisinger (Ed.), *Psychological testing of Hispanics.* Washington, DC: American Psychological Association.

Campos, L. P. (1989). Adverse impact, unfairness, and bias in the psychological screening of Hispanic peace officers. *Hispanic Journal of Behavioral Sciences, 11*, 127–135.

Casas, J. M. (1985). A reflection on the status of racial/ethnic minority research. *The Counseling Psychologist, 13*, 581–598.

Cataeno, R. (1986). Alternate definitions of Hispanics: Consequences of an alcohol survey. *Hispanic Journal of Behavioral Sciences, 8*, 35–40.

Cattell, R. B. (1940). A culture free intelligence test: Part I. *Journal of Educational Psychology, 31*, 161–179.

Chavez, E. L., & Gonzales-Singh, E. (1980). Hispanic assessment: A case study. *Professional Psychology: Research, Theory, and Practice, 11*, 163–168.

Cole, N. S. (1981). Bias in testing. *American Psychologist, 36*, 1067–1077.

Cuellar I., Harris, L. C., & Jasso, R. (1980). An acculturation scale for Mexican American normal and clinical populations. *Hispanic Journal of Behavioral Sciences, 2*, 99–217.

Dahlstrom, W. G., Lachar, D., & Dahlstrom, L. E. (Eds.). (1986). *MMPI patterns of American minorities*. Minneapolis: University of Minnesota Press.

Darlington, R. B. (1971). Another look at 'cultural fairness.' *Journal of Educational Measurement, 9*, 71–82.

Davis, C., Haub, C., & Willette, J. (1983). U.S. Hispanics: Changing the face of America. *Population Bulletin, 38*, 3.

Dunn, L. M., & Dunn, L. M. (1981). *Peabody picture vocabulary test-revised*. Circle Pines, MN: American Guidance Service.

Duran, R. P. (1989). Assessment and instruction of at-risk Hispanic children. *Exceptional Children, 56*, 154–158.

Eyde, L. D. (1992). Introduction to the testing of Hispanics in industry and research. In K. F. Geisinger (Ed.), *Psychological testing of Hispanics* (pp. 167-171). Washington, DC: American Psychological Association.

Eyde, L. D., Moreland, K. L., Robertson, G. J., Primoff, E. S., & Most, R. B. (1988). Test user qualifications: A data-base approach to promoting good test use. *Issues in scientific psychology.* Report of the Test User. Qualifications Working Group of the Joint Committee on Testing Practices (Research Report No. 89-01). Washington, DC: American Psychological Association.

Figueroa, R. A. (1989). Psychological testing of linguistic minority students: Knowledge gaps and regulations. *Exceptional Children, 56,* 145–152.

Fradd, S. H., & Correa, V. I. (1989). Hispanic students at risk: Do we abdicate or advocate? *Exceptional Children, 2,* 105–110.

Gatewood, R., & Perloff, R. (1990). Testing and industrial application. In G. Goldstein & M. Hersen (Eds.), *Handbook of psychological assessment* (2nd ed.). New York: Pergamon Press.

Goldman, S. R., & Trueba, H. T. (Eds.). (1987). *Becoming literate in English as a second language.* Norwood, NJ: Ablex.

Greene, R. L. (1987). Ethnicity and MMPI performance: A review. *Journal of Consulting Clinical Psychology, 55,* 497–512.

Holland, J. L. (1971). *The counselor's guide to the self-directed search.* Palo Alto, CA: Consulting Psychologists Press.

Holland, J. L. (1979). *The self-directed search professional manual.* Palo Alto, CA: Consulting Psychologists Press.

Ibrahim, F. A., & Arredondo, P. M. (1986). Ethical standards for cross-cultural counseling: Counselor preparation, practice, assessment, and research. *Journal of Counseling and Development, 64,* 349–352.

Kaplan, B., Rickers-Ovsiankina, M. A., & Joseph, A. (1956). An attempt to sort Rorschach records from four cultures. *Journal of Projective Techniques, 20,* 172–180.

Kuder, G. F., & Diamond, E. E. (1979). *Kuder occupational interest survey: General manual* (2nd ed.). Chicago: Science Research Associates.

Leal, A. (1990). Hispanics and substance abuse: Implications for rehabilitation counselors. *Journal of Applied Rehabilitation Counseling, 21,* 52–54.

Linskey, A., Arnold, B., & Hancock, S. (1983). Barriers to access and utilization of services by the handicapped Hispanic. In *The special rehabilitation and research needs of disabled Hispanic persons*. Edinburg, TX: National Institute of Handicapped Research and President's Committee on the Employment of the Handicapped.

Lonner, W. J. (1985). Issues in testing and assessment in cross-cultural counseling. *The Counseling Psychologist, 13,* 599–614.

Malgady, R. G., Rogler, L. H., & Costantino, G. (1987). Ethnocultural and linguistic bias in mental health evaluation of Hispanics. *American Psychologist, 42,* 228–234.

Montgomery, G. T., & Orozco, S. (1985). Mexican Americans' performance on the MMPI as a function of level of acculturation. *Journal of Clinical Psychology, 41,* 203–212.

Moore, J. (1990). Hispanic/Latino: Imposed label or real identity? *Latino Studies Journal, 1,* 33–47.

Murphy, L. L., Conoley, J. C., & Impara, J. C. (Eds.). (1994). *Tests in print IV: An index to tests, test reviews, and the literature on specific tests*. Lincoln: University of Nebraska Press.

National Commission on Testing and Public Policy. (1990). *From gatekeeper to gateway: Transforming testing in America*. Chestnut Hill, MA: Author.

Olmedo, E. L. (1977). Psychological testing and the Chicano: A reassessment. In J. L. Martinez Jr. (Ed.), *Chicano psychology* (pp. 175-195). New York: Academic.

Olmedo, E. L. (1981). Testing linguistic minorities. *American Psychologist, 36,* 1078–1085.

Ortiz, A. A., & Maldonado-Colon, E. (1986a). Recognizing learning disabilities in bilingual children: How to lessen inappropriate referrals of language minority students to special education. *Journal of Reading, Writing and Disabilities International, 43,* 47–56.

Ortiz, A. A., & Maldonado-Colon, E. (1986b). Reducing inappropriate referrals of language minority students to special education. In A. C. Willig & H. F. Greenberg (Eds.), *Bilingualism and learning disabilities: Policy and practice for teachers and administrators* (pp. 37-50). New York: American Library Publishing.

Padilla, A. M., & Ruiz, R. A. (1973). *Latino mental health: A review of the literature* (DHEW Publication No. HSM 73-9143). Washington, DC: U.S. Government Printing Office.

Padilla, E. R., & Lindholm, K. D. (1984). Hispanic behavioral science research: Recommendations for further research. *Journal of Behavioral Sciences, 6,* 13–32.

Padilla, E. R., Olmedo, E. L., & Loya, F. (1987). Acculturation and MMPI performance of Chicano and Anglo college students. *Hispanic Journal of Behavioral Sciences, 4,* 451–466.

Pennock-Roman, M. (1992). Interpreting test performance in selective admissions for Hispanic students. In K. F. Geisinger (Ed.), *Psychological testing of Hispanics* (pp. 99–135). Washington, DC: American Psychological Association.

Powers, S. (1982). *The effect of test-wiseness on the reading achievement scores of minority populations.* Final report. (ERIC Document Reproduction Service No. ED 222 549). Washington, DC: National Institute of Education.

Primoff, E. S., & Eyde, L. D. (1988). The job element method of job analysis. In S. Gael (Ed.), *The job analysis handbook for business industry and government* (pp. 807–824). New York: John Wiley & Sons.

Puente, A. E. (1990). Psychological assessment of minority group members. In G. Goldstein & M. Hersen (Eds.), *Handbook of psychological assessment* (2nd ed.). New York: Pergamon Press.

Ramos, R. A. (1981). Employment battery performance of Hispanic applicants as a function of English or Spanish test instructions. *Journal of Applied Psychology, 66,* 291–295.

Ramos, R. A. (1992). Testing and assessment of Hispanics for occupational and management positions: A developmental needs analysis. In K. F. Geisinger (Ed.), *Psychological testing of Hispanics.* Washington, DC: American Psychological Association.

Raven, J. F., Court, J. H., & Raven, J. (1985). *Manual for Raven's progressive matrices and vocabulary scales. Standard progressive matrices (Sec. 3).* London: HK Lewis.

Rueda, R. (1989). Defining mild disabilities with language-minority students. *Exceptional Children, 56,* 121–128.

Sandoval, J. (1979). The WAIS-R and internal evidence of test bias with a minority group. *Journal of Consulting and Clinical Psychology, 47,* 919–927.

Schmitt, A. P. (1988). Language and cultural characteristics that explain differential item functioning for Hispanic examinees on the Scholastic Aptitude Test. *Journal of Educational Measurement, 25,* 1–13.

Schmitt, A. P., & Dorans, N. J. (1991). Factors related to differential item functioning for Hispanic examinees on the Scholastic Aptitude Test. In D. Keller & R. J. Magallan (Eds.), *Assessment and access: Hispanics in higher education.* Albany, NY: State University of New York.

Shorris, E. (1992). *Latinos: A biography of the people.* New York: Norton.

Smart, J. F. (1993). Level of acculturation of Mexican Americans with disabilities and acceptance of disability. *Rehabilitation Counseling Bulletin, 36,* 199–211.

Smart, J. F., & Smart, D. W. (1992a). Cultural issues in the rehabilitation of Hispanics. *Journal of Rehabilitation, 58,* 29–37.

Smart, J. F., & Smart, D. W. (1992b). Curriculum changes in multicultural rehabilitation. *Rehabilitation Education, 6,* 105–122.

Smart, J. F., & Smart, D. W. (1993). Acculturation, biculturalism, and the rehabilitation of Mexican Americans. *Journal of Applied Rehabilitation Counseling, 24,* 46–51.

Sundberg, N. D., & Gonzales, L. R. (1981). Cross-cultural and cross-ethnic assessment: Overview and issues. In P. McReynolds (Ed.), *Advances in psychological assessment.* San Francisco: Jossey-Bass.

Szapocznik, J., Scopetta, M. H., Kurtines, W., & Arnalde, M. A. (1978). Theory and measurement of acculturation. *Inter-American Journal of Psychology, 12,* 113–130.

Thorndike, R. L. (1971). Concepts of culture fairness. *Journal of Educational Measurement, 8,* 63–70.

Valencia, R. R., & Rankin, R. J. (1985). Evidence of content bias on the McCarthy Scales with Mexican American children: Implications for test translation and nonbiased assessment. *Journal of Educational Psychology, 77,* 197–207.

Velasquez, R. J., & Callahan, W. J. (1991). Psychological testing of Hispanic Americans in clinical settings: Overview and issues. In K. F. Geisinger (Ed.), *Psychological testing of Hispanics* (pp. 253–265). Washington, DC: American Psychological Association.

Violato, C. (1984). The effects of Canadianization of American-based items on the WAIS and WAIS-R information subtests. *Canadian Journal of Behavioral Science, 16,* 36–41.

Watkins, C. E., Jr., & Campbell, V. L. (1990). Testing and assessment in counseling psychology: Contemporary development and issues. *The Counseling Psychologist, 18,* 189–197.

Winkler, K. J. (1990). Scholars say issues of diversity have revolutionized field of Chicano studies. *Chronicle of Higher Education, 37,* 4–9.

Wodarski, J. S. (1991). Social work practices with Hispanic Americans. In D. F. Harrison, J. S. Wodarski, & B. A. Thyer (Eds.), *Cultural diversity and social work practice* (pp. 71–105). Springfield, IL: C. C. Thomas.

Zeidner, M. (1988). Culture fairness in aptitude testing revisited: A cross-cultural parallel. *Professional Psychology: Research, Theory, and Practice, 19,* 257–262.

12

The Effective Use of Vocational Evaluation Services

Stephen W. Thomas, EdD, CVE, CRC

Dr. Thomas is Professor and Director, Graduate Program in Vocational Evaluation, Department of Rehabilitation Studies, East Carolina University, Greenville, NC.

KEY POINTS

- When vocational evaluation services are carefully chosen, the counselor will have a better chance of receiving information that will competently serve the planning process and assure client success.

- This chapter describes the primary considerations for systematically choosing appropriate vocational evaluation services, determining client readiness for referral, writing objective referral questions, and using evaluation reports in effective rehabilitation planning.

- Not every client needs a complete vocational evaluation. Vocational evaluations generally should be provided only when a client's occupational direction is in question. Routine vocational assessments conducted on all clients by rehabilitation counselors may be all that is needed to develop a rehabilitation plan.

- A difference exists between *vocational assessment* and *vocational evaluation*. Assessment is a less formal technique that is routinely provided throughout the life of a rehabilitation case. The accuracy of a good vocational assessment partly depends on the quality of a good vocational evaluation.

- The cornerstone of a quality vocational evaluation is two-way communication between the counselor and the evaluator.

INTRODUCTION

The effectiveness of vocational evaluation services has been well documented (Evans, 1986; Ward-Ross, 1985; Williams, 1975). Studies that compared success rates obtained when report recommendations were followed versus not followed suggest that vocational evaluation can make a significant difference in placement success when properly used in the rehabilitation planning process. Inadequate planning and placement outcomes can result, in part, from an improper evaluation and report or from a lack of counselor understanding of how to correctly choose and use evaluation services and reports. To help the counselor learn how to correctly use vocational evaluation services, this chapter describes the primary considerations for systematically choosing appropriate vocational evaluation services, determining client readiness for referral, writing objective referral questions, and using evaluation reports in effective rehabilitation planning. These procedures are important ingredients in improving the delivery of rehabilitation services.

A WORKING DEFINITION

Not every client needs a complete vocational evaluation. As surprising as this may sound, for the most part vocational evaluations should be provided only when a client's occupational direction is in question. Routine vocational assessments conducted on all clients by rehabilitation counselors may be all that is needed to develop a rehabilitation plan. However, if the assessment reveals a need for additional information, the counselor can choose the evaluation service (e.g., medical, psychological, educational, or vocational) that can best answer the question. To fully understand the difference between *vocational evaluation* and *vocational assessment*, the widely accepted definition by the Vocational Evaluation and Work Adjustment Association (VEWAA) will be used. Both the

Commission on Accreditation of Rehabilitation Facilities (CARF) and the Commission on Certification of Work Adjustment and Vocational Evaluation Specialists (CCWAVES) have adopted the following VEWAA definition of vocational evaluation:

> A comprehensive process that systematically uses work, either real or simulated, as the focal point for assessment and vocational exploration, the purpose of which is to assist individuals in vocational development. Vocational evaluation incorporates medical, psychological, social, vocational, educational, cultural, and economic data into the process to attain the goals of evaluation. (Dowd, 1993, p. 29)

Unique features of this definition that distinguish vocational evaluation from other evaluation services is its focus on "real and simulated" work and its broad inclusion of a variety of considerations that influence work such as medical, psychological, social, educational, cultural, and economic factors. It is important to keep in mind that vocational evaluation is much more than testing. If all clients and jobs were alike, then highly valid computerized test batteries would be in common use today. The fact is that the more subjective factors — motivation, interest, behavior, maturity, communication, and support — account for much of the variance in vocational decision making. Such factors cannot be easily measured by a computerized test battery and require "real or simulated" work environments to provide an accurate clinical assessment. Even the term *measure* is suspect, given the variability of people and jobs, and especially people with disabilities who now have greater access to job modification and accommodation under the law. This makes the use of clinical judgment within an ecological evaluation even more important today.

Assessment, on the other hand, is a less formal technique that is routinely provided throughout the life of a rehabilitation case (Corthell & Griswold, 1987). It begins when the application for services is reviewed and the client is met and ends with the close of the case. It is a multidisciplinary process that involves the coordination, collection, and analysis of formal evaluation data to assist in making planning decisions. It could involve observing client behaviors and characteristics during the initial meeting as well as reading and synthesizing a vocational evaluation report. The accuracy of a good vocational assessment depends in part on the quality of a good vocational evaluation. Vocational evaluation is part of the vocational assessment process and may not always be needed, depending on the utility of other assessment information.

CHOOSING A VOCATIONAL EVALUATION SERVICE

The rehabilitation counselor should take the time to carefully "evaluate" vocational evaluation services. Who would buy a car without first taking it for a test drive? Such caution should also apply when purchasing vocational evaluation services. Several important guidelines should be followed when determining the appropriateness of an evaluation service for a specific client. Not all vocational evaluation services work for every client. A short-term vocational evaluation (or vocational screening), ranging in length from several hours to several days, may yield pertinent information for individuals who are not severely disabled, or for persons who may already have established skills and abilities and simply need guidance to properly apply those skills in the right job or training program. On the other hand, persons with severe disabilities who have no vocational direction and have difficulty learning and generalizing information may need a long-term vocational evaluation that may last from several weeks to several months and rely on simulated and real work settings to modify and evaluate performance, behavior, and environmental considerations.

Many of the short-term services only have enough time to provide a diagnostic vocational evaluation—where the client is at the current time. Do not expect such services to provide detailed information on specific behavioral issues, stamina, performance improvement and maintenance, career exploration, and particular environmental accommodation and modification options. For example, how can a person's stamina to work an 8-hour-a-day, 5-day-a-week job be assessed in only a few hours? How can communication and cooperation skills with co-workers and supervisors be evaluated from an intake interview or with a standardized test? Although such evaluations are often attempted, they are of questionable value.

Services of a longer duration can frequently offer a prognostic vocational evaluation — *where the client could be* with specific services and accommodations. Time is needed in this latter evaluation process to assess behavior, accommodation needs and strategies, learning contingencies, performance improvement, and environmental considerations.

Evaluators in short-term evaluation settings often recommend a client be referred to long-term evaluation to further assess critical factors that could not be adequately addressed. The practice is no different from referrals made by family physicians to medical specialists when there is need for a more precise diagnosis and formulation of a specific plan of action. Short-term vocational evaluations provide an important service to a wide range of client populations; however, when clients have severe disabilities, the evaluations may not furnish all the essential information required for accurate planning. At times, they may only serve to screen out some clients who, with a more appropriate long-term evaluation, could receive better direction and opportunity for success.

Questions that should be addressed when determining the appropriateness of a vocational evaluation service include, but are not limited to:

- How severe is the client's disability and what are the information needs?

- What is the length of the evaluation service and what instruments and techniques are used?

- What can be expected from the vocational evaluation in terms of report content and outcomes?

- Is the evaluator competent to provide the desired service?

PREPARING FOR REFERRAL

Referral preparation, an often-overlooked phase, can make a difference in the success of a vocational evaluation. It requires that the rehabilitation counselor first determine if the client is currently appropriate for vocational evaluation services. Two areas of appropriateness must be determined: client readiness and client willingness (Thomas, 1990). *Client readiness* refers to the stability of the condition. If full medical and mental recovery is not achieved prior to referral, then the evaluation may only serve as a diagnostic, motivational, therapeutic, or career exploration tool. The presence of stability is often a difficult decision to make because stability of the condition requires subjective judgment, for example, when a person with traumatic brain injury or chronic depression would be ready for vocational evaluation. Vocational potential may be underestimated in such cases. On the other hand, delaying evaluation will lengthen rehabilitation cost and time and may diminish overall rehabilitation success (Bowe, 1986). When in doubt about the appropriate time of referral, consult the vocational evaluator. Communication between the counselor and evaluator is essential for ensuring appropriate referrals.

Determining *client willingness* is an equally complex process in establishing a client's readiness. It refers to the client's personal and emotional readiness to participate in a vocational evaluation. Persons who are experiencing difficulty in adjusting to their disability or are undergoing a personal crisis such as divorce, financial difficulties, court trial, or struggling to overcome substance abuse, may not be willing to explore vocational options until the problem is resolved. Again, vocational evaluation may refocus a client's attention to more positive life directions, but could result in an underestimation of vocational potential if the client is not fully committed to the process.

The level of client willingness can be ascertained and often improved through counseling and orientation. Counseling can be used to explore the client's commitment to entering and actively participating in evaluation. However, this requires orienting the client to what will happen in evaluation, what will result from the process, and how the results will be used in vocational preparation and placement. Some persons enter vocational evaluation with apprehension as a result of a lack of understanding or a misconception of what will happen. Some may think they will be "tested" or "trained" and will be fearful, anxious, or even suspicious of the process. The orientation should positively focus on clients' unique opportunities to explore their own personal interests and abilities as they relate to options for vocational training and job placement. Words such as "testing" should be avoided because they have a negative connotation. Emphasizing the client/evaluator partnership role will give the client a sense of ownership of the process, and may increase willingness to participate. Counselors may also wish to offer apprehensive clients a tour of the evaluation unit or supplement the orientation with printed materials and brochures on vocational evaluation in general and on the unit in particular.

WRITING REFERRAL QUESTIONS

One of the most important ways a counselor can communicate information needs to the vocational evaluator is through the referral question. The most typical referral directive asks the evaluator to find out everything possible about the client. However, more specific referral questions will ensure that primary information needs will receive special attention in evaluation. At times, counselors who are less than satisfied with evaluation results may find they did not take the time to ask a few simple referral questions. Counselors should feel free to request a comprehensive evaluation while asking for more detail in a few key areas. Specific questions may relate to identifying client interests and work values, work stamina, behavior, communication and cooperation, remedial needs, ability to return to a previous job, best instructional approaches, type of training best suited to the client, or transitional needs. Caution should be used in writing referral questions that cannot be answered by an evaluation unit because of program length or staff expertise and qualifications. In other words, do not ask for an assessment of work stamina from an evaluation of several hours or request a personality or mental status diagnosis from a unit not staffed by a licensed psychologist. When in doubt about the appropriateness of a referral or referral question, do not hesitate to consult the evaluator in charge of admissions. Prompt communication will save valuable time and money frequently lost through an unnecessary referral.

Whenever possible, include copies of special medical, psychological, or other pertinent evaluation reports or summaries, making sure that a consent for release of information form has been signed by the client. They may be crucial to writing recommendations that take into account all possible factors directly or indirectly related to the overall vocational potential of the client. In addition, evaluators place clients in a variety of physically and cognitively challenging and potentially stressful activities; knowing what situations to avoid will minimize the chance of harming the client.

WHAT TO EXPECT FROM THE VOCATIONAL EVALUATION PROCESS

Once a referral has been processed and accepted, the counselor and client will be notified of the start date. Immediately prior to the evaluation, the counselor must ensure the client will be attending, knows where to go and when to be there, and has dependable transportation to the unit. This minimizes "no-shows" that may place the client at the end of the waiting list. Again, any fears or apprehensions of the client about participating in evaluation should be discussed and resolved.

Although vocational evaluation approaches differ, a general outline of the process, from the client's perspective, will be presented to give some idea of what can be expected in terms of typical assessment strategies. Understanding the process will provide a better appreciation of — and the reasoning behind — the content of evaluation reports.

It is important to locate experienced and qualified evaluators who have the extensive knowledge and skills to offer a comprehensive, creative, and clinically oriented service. They should be able to modify instruments/techniques and accommodate and facilitate client performance. Facilities that are accredited by the CARF in vocational evaluation typically use qualified evaluators. Personnel that have been formally educated or extensively trained in vocational evaluation, or who are Certified in Vocational Evaluation (CVE) by CCWAVES, should be able to provide the quality service desired.

File Review:

Review of the client file inaugurates the evaluation process. Pertinent information garnered from the file is used to initially develop the individualized vocational evaluation plan (IVEP). The IVEP contains the referral questions as well as additional questions derived from the file review. The primary factors associated with each question, and the instruments and techniques needed to evaluate these factors, are the major content areas of the IVEP.

Information Questionnaire and Intake Interview:

Frequently, on admission, evaluees must complete an information questionnaire. This simulated job application form permits the evaluator to assess writing style, comprehension and written expression, ability to complete a job application form, and information on past and future aspirations. The questionnaire is used during the initial orientation and intake interview to help explain how the evaluation will specifically benefit the stated needs and aspirations of the client and to provide guidance in exploring critical information areas in greater detail. The intake interview will also facilitate assessment of job interviewing skills; general communication skills; initial behaviors and appearance; and responses to questions related to perceived strengths and needs, vocational history and goals, education, personal/social/family issues and supports, finances, disability and medications, hobbies and interests, and transition skills and needs. The interview may also be supplemented with a functional assessment of the evaluee's physical capacity and basic living skills.

Plan Revision:

The intake interview often is followed by a revision in the vocational evaluation plan to individually tailor the remaining process to the client's expressed needs. Plan revision is an ongoing process that changes as necessary. Depending on the severity of the disability and information needs, the evaluation may take several different directions.

Feasibility and Employability Phases:

For individuals with severe disabilities, a prevocational evaluation will be administered to assess current training or employment feasibility. It may include an assessment of interest and work values, basic skills, functional skills, achievement, aptitude, dexterity, and learning style. Results of the prevocational evaluation will determine if additional evaluation of employability skills is necessary or what additional services would be required prior to placement, training, or further evaluation. Persons who are not severely disabled may be given an assessment of interests and work values, achievement, aptitude, and dexterity.

Standardized tests are frequently used as a quick and reliable method to collect objective information on clients. However, because of poor reading levels, text anxiety, disability, accommodation needs, processing time, lack of realism and concreteness, and inappropriateness of many tests for use in rehabilitation settings, standardized tests do not always provide an accurate appraisal of a person's true ability. They tend to be limited primarily to vocational diagnosis (baseline establishment), and may instead screen clients out of further evaluation—and possibly out of the rehabilitation process as well. Therefore, the use of simulated and real-work instruments and techniques must be considered a more accurate evaluation of vocational potential and direction.

The employability phase incorporates many of the same instruments and techniques found in the feasibility phase, such as standardized tests and behavior observation, along with work samples, situational assessments, and job-site evaluation. Work samples are simulations of work tasks that possess psychometric properties of standardization (Pruitt, 1986). The clinical advantages of work samples over standardized tests include opportunities for interaction with the client, career exploration, modification and accommodation, evaluation of production improvement, observation of critical vocational behaviors, identification of work-related needs, and an analysis of criterion-referenced (content-specific) as well as norm-referenced performance (Thomas, 1991). Because of this flexibility, work sample evaluations take more time but provide a realistic assessment of work-related needs and capabilities. They are one of the better methods to evaluate the abilities of persons with severe disabilities who do not perform well on standardized tests (Power, 1991). Contingencies for improving performance and ensuring success can be prescribed through the creative use of work samples and work sample systems.

Situational assessment is a frequently used technique for

evaluating work-related behavior. This systematic but nonstandardized technique enables the evaluator to create work situations not always represented by work samples and often more characteristic of locally available jobs. For example, to assess a client's ability to perform and attend to tasks related to service occupations, an evaluator could direct the client to vacuum the floor or clean the windows in the unit. This would create an environment in which the client's behavior, memory, attention to task, decision-making skills, and general quality of work can be observed and reported. Modifications to enhance work speed, quality, or retention and recall can be applied to evaluate their overall impact on performance. Successful accommodations and adaptations can be discussed in the report as they relate to comparable changes in successful training or work.

Job site evaluation is the most valid and realistic technique for determining work potential. Because of the difficulty in developing and monitoring such sites, and the U.S. Department of Labor regulations requiring remuneration for any work that benefits employers, job-site evaluation is not frequently used. Placement and assessment in appropriate job sites is guided by previous evaluation findings and may last from several days to several weeks. Situational assessments and job site evaluations are more commonly used in long-term vocational evaluations and are primarily designed for use with persons who have severe disabilities.

COMMUNICATION AND VALIDATION

Vocational evaluation is often concluded with an exit interview. Clients are given an opportunity to express their opinions concerning the evaluation process as well as personal feelings about the types of work or training they might be willing to consider at this point in time. The evaluator synthesizes all of the information collected and formulates recommendations to be shared in the final staffing (optional) and written report. The staff often helps to refine results and reach a group consensus on client directions and alternatives that will be presented in the final report.

On average, vocational evaluation reports are sent to the referring counselor approximately 2 weeks from the date of client termination. The typical report contains four distinct sections: identifying information, the body of the report, summary and recommendations, and report attachments (optional appendices). "The identifying information establishes the client identity; the body of the report explains what happened during the evaluation and interprets, documents, and justifies the results; the summary abstracts what was written in the body of the report, and the recommendations identify plans of action; and the report attachments provide additional information on test/work sample descriptions and outcomes" (Thomas, 1986, p. 51). Depending on the length of the vocational evaluation, reports may vary in length from two to six pages, not including appendices.

Prescriptive Recommendations:

Special attention is paid to writing prescriptive recommendations, which spell out educational and vocational contingencies that must be addressed in the rehabilitation and placement process to improve chances for success. Examples of recommendations include, but are not limited to, the following types.

- *Placement*: Placement in jobs or training may be direct (no services needed), selective (selecting environments that fit the client), and descriptive (providing interventions, adaptations, or supported employment)

- *Education and training*: On-the-job training or apprenticeship; remedial, vocational, or formal education

- *Behavioral and emotional adjustment and counseling*: Personal therapy, social counseling, family therapy, work and career guidance

- *Independent living*: Transportation, housing, consumer skills, finances, recreation/leisure, community resource access, basic skills, grooming/ dress, and medical needs and services

- *Assistive technology*: Whatever is required at work or home or to provide transportation and security

- *Referral for additional evaluations*: Medical, educational, psychological, or assistive technology. needs

When recommendations require further explanation prior to use in planning, contact the evaluator for a consultation. Although report recommendations are the primary source for plan development information, the body of the report can provide detail regarding activities the client can perform, such as content descriptions of tests and work samples successfully completed. It also contains thorough descriptions of behavior, useful adaptations and modifications, and vocational assets and limitations. When these factors are incorporated into the Individualized Written Rehabilitation Program and thought-fully considered in the rehabilitation and placement process, the probability of success will be increased. If the content of the report does not meet assessment and planning needs, the rehabilitation counselor must work with the evaluator to modify the report to improve written communication of available evaluation information. Counselors must take the time to communicate to evaluators exactly what they want in written reports if they expect to receive helpful information. As a rule, vocational evaluators are flexible and try to meet the needs of the rehabilitation counselor, as long as they know what the counselor wants.

Follow-up:

Follow-up is an important concluding step in any quality evaluation process. Follow-up forms are either included with the report or sent to the counselor some time after the report has been mailed. Because these brief forms are used to improve evaluation services, it is in the counselor's best interest to objectively complete and return the form as soon as possible. Without this feedback, evaluators will not have the necessary information to make the required changes. However, if a counselor feels the evaluation or resulting report did not provide appropriate information to assist the planning process, then he or she should discuss this personally with the evaluator; future evaluations can then be tailored to meet the counselor's specific assessment and planning needs.

CONCLUSION

Vocational evaluation is a dynamic process that changes to meet the changing needs of each client. When evaluation services are carefully chosen, the counselor will have a better chance of receiving information that will competently serve the planning process and assure client success. Two-way communication between the counselor and evaluator is the cornerstone of a quality evaluation. Providing the evaluator with thorough client information and appropriate referral questions will ensure the receipt of a highly useful vocational evaluation report. When evaluations become a part of the counselor's service delivery process, opportunities to optimize client placement are increased. Together, the goal of improving the quality of life for persons with disabilities can be realized and client empowerment in the rehabilitation process achieved.

REFERENCES

Bowe, F. (1986). *Coming back: Directions for rehabilitation and disabled workers*. Hot Springs, AR: University of Arkansas, Research and Training Center in Vocational Rehabilitation.

Corthell, D. W., & Griswold, P. P. (Eds.) (1987). *Fourteenth institute on rehabilitation issues: The use of vocational evaluation in VR*. Menomonie, WI: University of Wisconsin-Stout, Research and Training Center.

Dowd, L. R. (Ed.). (1993). *Glossary of terminology for vocational assessment, evaluation, and work adjustment*. Menomonie, WI: Materials Development Center, University of Wisconsin-Stout.

Evans, L. (1986, December). *A study regarding performance in vocational classes of special needs students who received vocational assessments*. Paper presented to the Special Needs Division of the American Vocational Association, New Orleans, Louisiana.

Power, P. W. (1991). *A guide to vocational assessment* (2nd ed.). Austin, TX: Pro-Ed.

Pruitt, W. A. (1986). *Vocational evaluation* (2nd ed.). Menomonie, WI: Walt Pruitt Associates.

Thomas, S. W. (1986). *Report writing in assessment and evaluation*. Menomonie, WI. University of Wisconsin-Stout, Materials Development Center.

Thomas, S. W. (1990). Vocational assessment of multiple and severe physical impairments. In S. J. Scheer (Ed.), *Multidisciplinary perspectives in vocational assessment of impaired workers* (pp. 31-46). Rockville, MD: Aspen.

Thomas, S. W. (1991). *Vocational evaluation and traumatic brain injury: A procedural manual*. Menomonie, WI. University of Wisconsin-Stout, Materials Development Center.

Ward-Ross, L. E. (1985). *Contribution of vocational evaluators' recommendations to client rehabilitation success*. Unpublished masters thesis, East Carolina University, Greenville, N.C.

Williams, D. M. (1975). *A follow-up study on the relationship between work evaluators' recommendations and client placement.* Menomonie, WI: University of Wisconsin-Stout, Stout Vocational Rehabilitation Institute.

Name Index

A

B

C

D

Y

Z

Subject Index

Contributors

Catherine Clubb Foley, PhD
Assistant Professor, Department of Physical Medicine, and Senior
Researcher, the Center for Research on Women with Disabilities, Baylor
College of Medicine, Houston, TX.

Robert T. Fraser, PhD, CRC
Professor in the Department of Neurology, with joint appointments in
Neurological Surgery and Rehabilitation Medicine, University of
Washington; and Consultant, Associates in Rehabilitation and
Neuropsychology, Seattle, WA.

Cheryl Hanley-Maxwell, PhD
Associate Professor and Chair, University of Wisconsin-Madison,
Madison, WI.

H. Richard Lamb, MD
Professor of Psychiatry, University of Southern California School of
Medicine, Los Angeles, CA.

Cecile Mackota
Former Director of Vocational Rehabilitation, San Mateo County
(California) Mental Health Services, San Mateo, CA.

Garrett McAuliffe, PhD
Associate Professor of Counselor Education, Old Dominion University,
Norfolk, VA.

Margaret A. Nosek, PhD
Associate Professor, Department of Physical Medicine and Director of
the Center for Research on Women with Disabilities, Baylor College of
Medicine, Houston, TX.

Lewis E. Patterson, EdD
Professor Emeritus of Counseling, the College of Education at Cleveland State University, Cleveland, OH.

Jay W. Rojewski, PhD
Associate Professor, Department of Occupational Studies, The University of Georgia, Athens, GA.

James Schaller, PhD
Assistant Professor, The University of Texas at Austin.

Gary L. Sigmon, EdD
Vocational Consultant, Blue Ridge Vocational Services, Boone, NC.

Julie F. Smart, PhD, CRC, NCC, LPC, ABDA
Assistant Professor, Department of Special Education and Rehabilitation, Utah State University, Logan, UT.

David W. Smart, PhD
Professor, Counseling and Development Center, Brigham Young University, Provo, UT.

Edna Mora Szymanski, PhD,
Professor and Associate Dean, University of Wisconsin-Madison, Madison, WI.

Stephen W. Thomas, EdD, CVE, CRC
Professor and Director, Graduate Program in Vocational Evaluation, Department of Rehabilitation Studies, East Carolina University, Greenville, NC.

David Vandergoot, PhD, CRC
President, the Center for Essential Management Services, Oceanside, NY; and Faculty Member, Hunter College, New York, NY.

Rock Weldon, MA, CVE
Vocational Consultant, Weldon & Associates, Greenville, SC.

For information on other books in
The Hatherleigh Guides series, call the
Marketing Department at Hatherleigh
Press, 1-800-367-2550, or write:
Hatherleigh Press
Marketing Department
1114 First Avenue, Suite 500
New York, NY 10021-8325